Are you MAD *at me?*

Understanding and Dealing with the *GAMES* GirlFriends Play!

Between Friends

PUBLISHING

SHIRLEY ANNE TULLIO

Scripture is taken from The New American Standard Bible. Copyright 1960, 1962, 1963, 1968, 1971, 1972, 1973, 1975, 1977, 1995. Used by permission. (www.Lockman.org)

Scripture quotations from the Holy Bible, New Living Translation, copyright 1996, 2004. Used by permission of Tyndale House Publishers. Wheaton, Illinois 60189. All rights reserved.

Scripture taken from The Message Copyright 1 1993, 1994, 1995, 1996, 2000, 2001, 2002. Used by permission of NavPress Publishing Group.

Scripture quotations from Amplified Bible, copyright 1954, 1958, 1962, 1964, 1965, 1987 The Lockman Foundation. Used by permission. (www.Lockman.org)

Scripture taken from The Holy Bible, New International Version, copyright 1973, 1978, 1984, 2010 Biblica.

Cover and Logo Design by FayeFayeDesigns at Fiverr.com

Published by: *Between Friends Publishing*, Bradenton, Florida.

BFPShirleyAnne@gmail.com

ISBN: 9780578-71249-9

LCCN: 2020911014

Printed in the United States of America

I dedicate this book to:

All My GirlFriends

Who I Have Ever Been Mad at,
and
Whoever Have Been Mad at Me!

I Have Changed Your Names
to
Protect the Guilty,
and
You Know Who You are!

Thank you, and God Bless You All!

Contents

Introduction

We've all heard the children's nursery rhyme that claims, *"Sticks and Stones may break my bones, but names will never hurt me."* Are you kidding me? Obviously, the person who wrote this little jingle was *NOT* a Girl! Skinny minny, four eyes, dummy, ugly duckling, and those are just some of the names my little girlfriends called me. If you have ever been called names, talked about, yelled at, or lied about, then you know that words definitely *CAN* hurt you.

Of course, most of our GirlFriends wouldn't say or do any of those things to us now, or would they? As grown-ups, I would *LOVE* to say we don't need to deal with issues like these anymore, but unfortunately, I would be wrong. (Listen up, because you won't hear me say that too often). What I have found to be true though, are those same awful *feelings* when a GirlFriend is mean to you, gets mad at you or when you get mad at her.

From the sandboxes on the playgrounds of yesterday, to the shopping malls of today, some things never seem to change. The loneliness, rejection, betrayal, and feelings of anger, being unloved or misunderstood are horrific! It's actually because of my going through hurtful experiences like these, I write this book. But we'll get to that later.

I would also *LOVE* to say, we in our church environments are immune to similar situations as these, but again, I would be wrong! (I really don't like the way this is going.) I was a Pastor's wife for nearly 25 years, a Women's Ministry Director, Bible Teacher,

Event Speaker, Business Owner, and have been abundantly blessed with hundreds of GirlFriends over the years.

It also means I've had my share of *issues* with GirlFriends as well. Let me just say here, not one of them was perfect, nor am I. That doesn't excuse us; it just explains that we are *ALL* still in the process of being "Conformed to the image and likeness of Christ." Romans 8:2

It's sad to say, but we are living in a mad, mad, a realllly *MAD* world these days. Even more so, than when I began writing this book a few years ago. Sure, name-calling still hurts, it always has and always will. However, we have taken this *madness* to a whole nother level of nastiness. We call it bullying, character assassination, intimidation, harassment, and it's not just for kids anymore.

We witness this daily on the news, and even on certain popular tv shows, where we observe the Mean Girls, the Bad Girls, the Gossip Girls, and all those crazy Housewife Girls of every county, and some other girls I'd rather not mention here! They've become our new, and *un*-improved role models, getting in each other's faces, flipping tables, and talking bad *to* and *about* each other.

To add insult to injury, they actually get paid to act this way! It doesn't stop there with just those girls, either. 2 Timothy 3:2-4 warns us by saying, "There will be times when many people will be out of control, lovers of self and money, ungrateful, boastful, treacherous, rash, disobedient to their parents, gossipers, slanderers, unforgiving," and the list goes on. One version even uses the word *brutal* to describe the way people will behave!

Unfortunately, I believe we are in those days right now. We are getting *mad* at each other on our highways, in the workplace and on our kid's soccer fields. This craziness is even being played out in our used-to-be safe churches, schools, and neighborhoods. I could go on and on, but I won't, because we must *choose* to *focus* on being the *change*, not being *fixated* on all the *deranged*. Whew!

Come on now GirlFriends, let's do our part to stop all this *madness*. We have a seemingly small, although significant, role to play in influencing others for good, in whatever corner of the world God has placed us in. He has called us to be the Peacemakers, not the Troublemakers, as it relates to our GirlFriends! There *IS* a way to enjoy the blessings of Girlfriends, *IF* we choose to deal with one another God's way. I know that's what you want, because you picked up this book.

Whenever we act like some of those self-centered, *mad* little kids we've all witnessed in our grocery stores and beyond, we are playing right into the hands of the enemy. 1 Corinthians 11:13 tells us, "When we were children, we spoke like a child, understood as a child, and thought as a child. When we grow up, we are to put away childish things." Those *things* Paul is referring to, include all those not so nice *Games* we sometimes play while interacting with our GirlFriends.

So, What's a Girl to DO?

As in any *Game* we play in life, there must be a set of rules to follow. If not, there would be utter chaos everywhere, which is exactly the reason why so many of us are getting asked that question by our GirlFriends. You know the one I mean. *"Are You Mad at Me?"* Don't you just hate that? I know I do. Whenever anyone asks me that, I actually begin to physically sweat!

My mind goes to everything I could possibly have said or done to offend her. Or maybe she did or said something to offend me? Am I *mad* at her or is she *mad* at me? Well, my new favorite response to that dreaded question has become, "*Should I be?*" It gives me time to take a deep breath, and settle down my racing heart and mind before answering. You can use it too, it's free! However, be very prepared, because she will more than likely tell you!

The *Good News* is we don't need to reinvent the wheel. We have already been given The GirlFriend's *rules* for good behavior. They are all found in God's Word, and the best part is they work, *IF* we follow them. Now, I am *NOT* saying there is some kind of magical 1-2-3 step formula, and instantly every relationship will now become perfect.

Obviously, we can *NOT* control another person's emotions, thoughts, actions, or reactions, despite how hard we might try. Should we repeat that? Say it with me, now. We can *NOT* control another person's emotions, thoughts, actions, or reactions, no matter how hard we try. Right? And oh, how we have tried! How, might I ask, has that been workin' for you so far? That's what I thought.

My advice on that subject would be to say: Just *STOP* trying! Heck, we can barely control our own selves at times. But, I can say with confidence, by following these guidelines, you can experience deeper and longer lasting friendships, and a whole lot more fun while doing it. The added bonus, when following God's principles is, we will also get to enjoy a sense of peace, knowing we are striving to obey and please Him. We'll talk more about how to specifically do that in later chapters.

In Part 1, we will Discuss the different types of friendships, Discover what to look for in a friend, and be Challenged to be a true friend who sticks closer than a 'sister', in good times and in bad.

We'll deal in Part 2 with that *Elephant* in the middle of the room, be Honest about Gossip, Get a Grip on Control, and Learn how to Handle Anger, Jealousy, and Rejection. Finally, in Part 3, we'll Uncover the true meanings of Love and Forgiveness.

Let me just mention here, even though I have written this book specifically for our GirlFriend relationships, these principles can be very effective in dealing with all our other interactions, as well.

Now, you can read this book in two ways. First, you can simply read it like any other book, and hopefully be Entertained, Encouraged, and Enlightened a bit, and that would be GOOD. IF you prefer to enhance your experience by making some real-life changes, you can intentionally apply the *rules* of each *Game* to your friendships, which I believe would be BEST. IF you decide to choose the latter, I would suggest you do the following:

- *PRAY* before reading each chapter. Ask God to reveal those attitudes or behaviors in your life that need *tweaking*.
- *HIGHLIGHT* areas you believe God is zeroing in on in your life. You'll recognize those areas because you may feel 'guilty', in a good way. Remember, He loves you where you are, but He loves you too much to leave you there!
- Throughout the chapter, you will be given personal reflection questions. *RESPOND* to each as honestly as possible. There are no right or wrong answers because they're exclusive to you.
- Be *INTENTIONAL*. Write out a specific *Game* plan of action of changes you want to make.

- Take *ACTION.* Do what's needed to make those changes. Unfortunately, transformation doesn't happen overnight, but one step at a time will bring you closer to your goal.

You may have already noticed on occasion, I have changed the word 'he', as used in the Bible, to 'she'. Please don't be *mad* at me for doing this. I only adjusted them temporarily to make the verses more personal and relatable to GirlFriends. Ready? Here comes the next one.

James 1:22-25 talks about the 'girl' who hears the Word of God, but does nothing about it. "Be DOERS of the Word, not hearers only. 'She' is like the person who looks at 'her' face in the mirror, goes away, and immediately forgets what kind of 'woman she' saw. She deceives 'herself'." The promise immediately after is, "IF you DO what God and His Word says, you will be blessed in all you do." I love a great deal as much as the next person, and being blessed for doing the right thing sounds like an offer too good to refuse!

So, how was that? I know there were a lot of words to change. You have my permission to cross my 'she's' out and put the 'he's' back in if it makes you feel more comfortable. I get that!

As we uncover each of the *Games* GirlFriends play, my goal would be to:

1. **Identify** each *Game.*

2. **Teach** you *the Rules.* Remember, *IF* you don't know what *The Manual says*, you could needlessly hurt yourself, and others too!

3. **Encourage** you and your GirlFriends to become *Real Game Changers* by playing the friendship *Game* together ~ God's way.

If you want to have even more fun, invite a group of your GirlFriends to take this journey along with you. However, make your choices wisely. I will say no more regarding that!

Now, Get Ready.....Set.....here we GO!

PART 1

*** *Girl Friends Rule* ***

God has Called Us

to be the

Peacemakers

Not the Troublemakers

CHAPTER 1
It's Such a Girl Thing!

"A 'girl' who has friends must show 'herself' to be friendly."

Proverbs 18:24

Ahhh....GirlFriends! To paraphrase a quote by C S Lewis: *"Friendships are born when one girl says to another girl, 'Oh my gosh, you too?' I thought I was the only one who felt that way."* Isn't that the truth! For me personally, I don't know who, what or where I would be today without my GirlFriends.

Even though I've been married to a wonderful man for many years, I don't care what anyone says, it's still not the same as having GirlFriends. Despite the recent denials in today's world, women are just plain and simply different than men. Case in point. Firstly, with my GirlFriends, I don't feel pressured to give them the short version of one of my stories. Secondly, there's no need to explain to them what on earth I'm talking about. You know that sometimes puzzled, glazed-over look we see on a man's face right in the middle of one of our *dissertations*? We seldom, if ever, see that same expression while *sharing* with a GirlFriend. They just *get us*, if you know what I mean. Of course you do ~ you're a GIRL!

Many studies have shown the average woman uses approximately 20,000 words a day, give or take a couple thousand. However, a typical man speaks about 7,000 words a day, and that's *only* if you ask him lots of questions! So, if my math is correct, that would be 13,000 *MORE* words women speak each and every day than men. Now you see why having GirlFriends is really not an option. We absolutely *NEED* them!

I think it's easy sometimes to either idealize or even devalue the importance of having GirlFriends. However, I do believe spending time with good friends can truly be some of life's most rewarding and fulfilling experiences. Don't you agree? I will also say, they can be some of life's most challenging, frustrating, and heartbreaking times we get to deal with too. I think we would all shout an "*Amen*" to that!

Researchers likewise have proven friendships can have a huge, positive impact on our health and happiness too. Maintaining a close circle of friends can relieve stress, prevent isolation, loneliness, and provide comfort and encouragement to us. A recent study even found having a *tribe* can add a significant number of years to our lives too! I think chocolate does all that as well, but then again, it adds on all those extra, unwanted pounds too! Well, that's an issue we'll discuss perhaps in my next book.

Before going any further, let's hear what Mr. Webster has to say concerning friends.

DEFINITION of a FRIEND:

* One attached to another by affection or esteem.

* A favored companion.

* A person who knows you well and is fond of you.

* A supporter or sympathizer.

* A person on the same side in a struggle.

* One that is not hostile. (Uh, let's hope not!)

* She always has a stash of chocolates she's willing to share! Ooops sorry, I was getting a bit ahead of myself. That goes on the next line below.

What is your personal definition of a GirlFriend?

_____

It's not just me, research or science which recognizes the true value of friendships, God is all about *connections* too. It's the reason He sent Jesus to earth, so we could have a personal relationship with Him. The Bible confirms this importance in Ecclesiastes 4:9 when it states: "Two can accomplish more than twice as much as one. If one falls, the other pulls 'her' up, but if one falls alone, 'she' is in trouble. One standing alone can be attacked and defeated, but two can stand back to back can and conquer. Three is even better; for a three-strand cord is not easily broken."

Wow, such a great picture of what a real GirlFriend looks like. She has your back, and you have hers. I've seen this in action so many times in my life with all my amazing GirlFriends, I could write an entire book on the subject. Oh, I just did! Having said that, I can also remember a season in my life when this was not what I was experiencing. Knowing you, as I obviously do, you too have probably been in situations where you were not *feelin' the love* from a GirlFriend either.

One of my most challenging times was when my husband and I decided to uproot our family and move to Florida. Up to that point, we had always lived in the same city, along with both of our families and all our friends. We were excited to begin this new adventure, even though we were totally unfamiliar with the area, we didn't know one soul, nor did either of us have jobs. I would definitely not encourage anyone to take that same course of action as we did. What were we thinking?

I guess we were thinking of getting away from those long winters, and lake effect snows of Erie, Pa., which could last well into Spring. It was not like we were running away from anyone or anything negative, except for that of course. Instead, we believed we were *moving* towards something new, fresh, and the good plan God had for us. Sounds like fun, right? I must say, I'm thankful we don't always know what He has planned for us ahead of time. I think if we did, many of us would choose to stay in our *comfort zones*, myself included.

So, we pressed forward and made our step by step plans to move after our two oldest children graduated from high school. Check. We sold our house and pretty much everything in it. Check. We said our tearful goodbyes to everyone and everything we held dear. Check. Then, slowly made the 22-hour journey down to our new home which was being built.

At that time, I was blessed with a husband of 20 years who loved me, three beautiful, healthy kids, our lovely new home, my YOUTH (which I think I miss the most, or is it my mind?) and the best part was that I had Jesus in my life. I loved Him, and He loved me. I had so much to be grateful for, which I was, yet I was still feeling as if something was missing. I just wasn't happy. Have you ever felt that way?

Name a time in your life when you had many external blessings yet still felt empty.

What do you think was missing?

On most days, it was difficult for me to even get motivated to get out of bed! I told myself no one would notice or really care anyway. This would have been the perfect opportunity for me to practice "Taking every thought captive" 2 Corinthians 10:5, or to count my many blessings, rather than my losses. I didn't!

It might be helpful for you to understand something here. Prior to this life-changing move, I had never been depressed. Generally speaking, I was the person who had always encouraged my GirlFriends to trust God when they were experiencing difficult times. It was me who was the great advice giver, offering them my wise counsel of how they could not only *survive but thrive'* during those times.

Now, I was the one on the other side of the couch who was wallowing in my own self pity. I was the girl who forgot to look in the mirror and give myself that same encouragement I had so readily given to my GirlFriends. I had simply abandoned what I knew was the right thing to do. Because of that, it was *ME* who was suffering. I couldn't even follow my own advice. What was wrong with me?

Just a little tip here. *NEVER*, ever, ask yourself that question, under any circumstance. Trust me when I tell you, your brain is like Google, and will come up with many answers to that 'innocent' question. It will systematically inform you of all the things that are wrong with you, whether they're true or not! However, the most important opinions of you are not the ones coming from Google, your GirlFriends or anyone else, for that matter. They are the truths of what God says about you, and the beliefs you have of yourself, which will influence your life the most! I'm just sayin'.

Now, most people will experience a down day or two when a situation gets the best of them. But what I was experiencing was occurring day after day, week after week, and month after month. I did my best to take positive steps to try to pick myself *up* by attending church regularly, which made me cry. I listened to worship music, which also made me cry. I even went to several different ladies' groups, which made me miss the ease of being with my old GirlFriends even more!

Let me just say here, dear GirlFriends, if you are experiencing similar, persistent feelings as I just described, I would advise you to seek professional help. Below is a recent list from the American Psychological Association, which includes some of the most common symptoms of depression:

Sad for a long period of time

Mood swings

Sleeping or eating changes

Feeling a sense of worthlessness

Less interested in doing activities you enjoyed prior

Little or no energy

Social isolation

Inability to concentrate

Sense others would be better off without you

It's a normal reaction to feel sad, lonely, or *down* when you have personal losses, life's struggles, or an injured self-esteem. However, when these feelings become overwhelming and life altering, you are more than likely experiencing *'clinical depression'*. You would do well to speak to a doctor, mental health care specialist or your pastor, as soon as possible. I don't claim to be any of those, but one thing I know for sure is, you need to get some good counsel and relief, and I'm happy to say they are readily available to you today.

No matter who you are or what is going on in your life right now, if you have a heartbeat, then God still has an awesome plan and purpose for you. I hope you realize that there *is* an enemy, he *is* real, and is looking to do whatever he can to thwart that great design for you. He knows keeping you *stuck* and depressed will deter you from ever accomplishing any of it.

My only regret is I didn't do that myself. Because of my own ignorance and pride, I believe I suffered much longer than I needed to. Thirty years ago, when I was experiencing this, seeking counseling had a very negative stigma attached to it. As a Christian, I believed to solicit any help outside of God and prayer, was a sign of spiritual weakness. Not only did I believe that, but that same sentiment was expressed to me from other well-meaning people I knew too.

Besides, when others looked at my 'perfect' life on the outside, who was going to feel sorry for me, besides *ME*? I figured the best solution, at that time, was to try to *get over it,* and *suck it up and deal with it,* all on my own. That did not work very well for me, and I have a hunch it will not be in your best interest either. Like the American poet, Maya Angelou said: "*When you know better, then you DO better!* "

I'm happy to say, most of us today embrace seeking emotional and mental help, and view it as an indication of strength, rather than weakness. So, be strong and courageous GirlFriend, and reach out to someone now for guidance soon. You'll be *happy* you did. BTW, did you know when you rearrange the letters in the word *depression* you will find the uplifting words of "*I pressed on*". Guess you could say: Sometimes it's all in how we choose to look at things!

Anyway, an important detour: now back to our story ~

To add insult to injury, even our 13-year-old daughter, Joy, was struggling with similar feelings as I was having. Perhaps you know what that's like when your child is hurting, and *YOU* are the one responsible. No, not on purpose, of course. Nevertheless, she was still deeply impacted by our choices.

We both wanted to return to the comforts of our home in Pennsylvania, to our family, friends, former church, fulfilling career, familiar stores, and well ~ everything! Then one day it happened! Joy connected with her first GirlFriend. Her name was 'Tina'. I was concerned because she was a few years older than Joy, and I hoped, a little wiser. To be honest, I think she may have hung out at our house initially because of Joy's very handsome (if I might say so myself) two older brothers, Mike and Steve! It worked out perfectly though, as 'Tina' became like a big sister to her, and introduced her to girls at church, who were more age appropriate.

Whenever 'Tina' came over, she would always say: *"Mrs. T, you really need to meet my mother, 'Carolyn'. You two are so much alike, I know you would become best friends."* That was it! That was the missing piece of the puzzle I had been searching for. A new Best Friend! Someone I could be myself with, laugh and cry with, shop with, pray with, have tea and chocolate with, not necessarily in that order. Casually, I said to her *"Have her give me a call sometime."* After a couple weeks passed, 'Carolyn' *did* call me.

We enjoyed a wonderful time of sharing. I think we used up all of our 20,000 words and a portion of the next day's quota, all in that one conversation. It was fun having someone who talked as fast as I did, and the cool part was we understood each other too. 'Tina' was right, we did have much in common and for the first time, I felt excited at the potential of having a new Best Friend.

At the end of our two-hour conversation, 'Carolyn' said: "*Can I be really honest with you?*" I was like, *"Sure"*. I was thinking she must have felt the same way I did too. Then, she spoke those words I will *NEVER forget*. She said ~ Wait for it ~

"*I hope you don't take this personally, or in the wrong way, but honestly, I just don't have time for any more friends in my life.*" Wow, talk about kicking a girl when she is down! Like any good Christian girl would say, I forced out these 'spiritually correct', yet untrue words: "*Of course not, no worries, I totally understand.*" And shortly after that disclosure of her discouraging words, we ended the conversation. I ran to my bedroom, slammed shut the door behind me, and burst into tears. I was back in bed, covers up over my head.

I guess I had assumed wrong. Now, I was feeling worse than I had prior to speaking with her. The hurt and rejection from her words had deepened my already sad and lonely heart. I was *mad* at her, and *mad* at myself for hoping things could be any different than they already were for me.

Have you ever felt that way or was it just me? Why was I acting like that teenage girl I was sooo many years prior? It's really simple ~ because we were made for close relationships. I really *needed* a GirlFriend, especially during that time in my life.

Shortly after my 'woe is me' spree, I crawled up out of the pits and realized that in order to move forward in this new venture, I needed to let go of my yearnings for my old life, and stop striving to be happy in my new one. I made the decision to start refocusing on being the best wife, mother, and woman I could be, exactly where I was, with or without GirlFriends. It was a time of trusting God completely to give me whatever or whoever He saw fit during that season in my life. "My God will supply all your needs according to His riches in glory by Christ Jesus." Philippians 4:19

BTW, God had a different plan for 'Carolyn'. She and I have been BFF's for over 30 years! I recently mentioned that conversation to her again. She said she still doesn't remember it. However, realizing how much it impacted me, she apologized for it again. Of course, I forgave her.....again! You'll love this one. Several times over the years she has said to me, "*I just don't know what I would do without you.*" My response to her has always been the same. "*Well, you almost found out!*"

So, What's a Girl to DO?

Friendships are not always easy to find or maintain. It takes time and effort to make new connections. It also means putting yourself out there, which can be intimidating, especially if you have been hurt by a GirlFriend. Besides taking the initial leap of faith of making new friends, developing lasting friendships must be intentional. Here are a few ways to *BEhave,* in order to maintain healthy friendships:

BE Real

BE Loyal

BE Loving

BE Yourself

BE Sensitive

BE Forgiving

BE Thoughtful

BE Encouraging

BE Understanding

Circle your greatest strengths.

Place a check next to the one(s) you wish to improve on.

Did you know there are approximately 100 *"one another"* exhortations in the Bible? Here are a few ways God wants us to relate to our GirlFriends and others.

*Bear one another's burdens. Galatians 6:2

*Pray for one another. James 5:16

*Be at peace with one another. Mark 9:50

*Honor one another. Romans 12:10

*Accept one another. Romans 15:7

*Serve one another. Galatians 5:13

*Be patient with one another. Ephesians 4:2

*Forgive one another. Ephesians 4:32

*Encourage one another. Hebrews 10:25

*Confess your sins to one another. James 5:16

So, we've talked about the value, purpose, and blessings of having GirlFriends in our lives. Now, let me ask you this question: Do you think it really matters to God what kind of GirlFriends we choose to have? Well, His Word has some pretty strong things to say concerning those choices.

Even while growing up, our parents cautioned us regarding the importance of the friends we chose. They said, "*Birds of a feather, flock together.*" We *will* become like those we *fly* with! Here are a few warnings to heed from God's Word, which are given for our protection.

1 Corinthians 15:33. Bad company corrupts character.

Proverbs 13:20. Walk with the wise and become wise, for a companion of a fool suffers harm.

Psalm 1:1 Blessed is the woman who walks not in the counsel of the wicked, nor stands in the way with sinners, nor sits in the seats of mockers.

Proverbs 22:24-25 Make no friendship with a 'woman' given to anger.

Proverbs 16:28-29 One who hurts people with bad talk separates the best of friends.

1Corinthians. 5:11 "Don't associate with one who is guilty of sexual immorality, or is greedy, worships idols, abuses others with their words, gets drunk, or cheats; don't even eat with people like that.

To me, not having real GirlFriends in my life, would be like having chocolate chip cookies, but without the chips! What good would that be? I honestly love the ones with the *nuts* best ~ both my cookies and my friends! They sure do make our lives a whole lot richer, sweeter, and *FUN*!

Before we explore the specific not so nice *Games* we sometimes play, let's first have a look at several of the different types of GirlFriends we may have encountered over the years.

Hold onto your hats, GirlFriends, we could be in for a bumpy ride ahead!

Most GirlFriends

are Not

Looking for Perfection,

They are

Merely Desiring

Connection.

CHAPTER 2
The Blessings of Girl Friends!

"A friend loves at all times, and a 'sister' is born for adversity."

Proverbs 17:17

I don't believe any GirlFriend comes into our lives by accident or coincidence, but rather it's God who brings her across our path. Some may enter and stay forever, while others only visit for a season; but either way, it's always for a reason. They can teach us about Who He is, and also reveal to us who we really are. Some will bring out the best in us like our gifts and confidence, however, there are other girls who will uncover hidden attitudes and insecurities in us we didn't even realize were there!

In this chapter we will identify the characteristics of several of these types of GirlFriends, and touch on some of the *unfriendly Games* we play with one another. As the stages of our lives change, we'll see how certain friendships overlap or shift from one category to another. To make it more personal, you may want to write your GirlFriend's name next to the kind of friend she is to you. You'll also notice how no two friendships are the same, for obvious reasons. No two girls are alike!

I hope you will observe by the end of this chapter, how blessed you've been by the women who have lifted you up and cheered you on along your journey. If that's not what you find, hang in there and be encouraged, because that GirlFriend could be just around the corner, waiting to meet you.

Ok, let's start on a positive note with the best kinds of GirlFriends we all want, and hopefully aspire to be.

FOREVER FRIEND

This is the girl who shows up for you! She knows your heart's desires, strengths, and weaknesses. She doesn't compete with you, but rather cheers you on in your successes. She always encourages you whenever you fall short. She will pray *with* you and *for* you, but *NEVER* about you. She's the GirlFriend who *cracks up* at the dumbest things you say or do, which sometimes aren't even funny, except to the two of you.

You've done real life together in the valleys and on the mountain tops. She's an iron sharpens iron kind of GirlFriend as she challenges you to be better. You've been through it all together, the thick and thin of it, and I mean that literally! You have prayed for each other's family members by name. You've stayed up late into the night in deep conversations, solving yours and everyone else in the world's problems.

You're able to complete each other's sentences, which can be a bit irritating at times, but mostly fun. You trust her with your story, and are confident she won't share it with anyone else, without your permission. Sometimes she may not support a decision you make, but she will always love and support *you*.

Even if you don't see each other as often as you'd like, you know she is always there for you. She gives you the freedom to be yourself, imperfections and all. Your Forever Friend has stood the test of time. She is like family, and sometimes even closer. She knows you best, yet still loves you. She's your BFF!

IF you have ever had even *ONE* GirlFriend like this, you are indeed blessed. If you long for this type of Friend, it usually doesn't happen overnight, that's not to say it can't. However, generally speaking, a Forever Friend takes quality and quantity time, nourishment, and it must be intentional and reciprocal.

This description reminds me of my very first Forever Friend in the whole wide world. I hope this story helps you see this kind of friendship in a simple, innocent, and uncomplicated way.

Nancy and I lived a couple houses from each other growing up. We did everything together. We attended the same elementary school and church. We played Canasta on her front porch every day in the summer. We even produced backyard 'shows', where we twirled batons, performed cartwheels, and spun hula hoops around our then tiny little waists (hers still is, mine, not so much). The neighborhood kids actually paid real money to see our acts, and we took it!

Along with my sister, Jeanne, we sang *'Let me go Lover'* on a local TV talent show. We definitely were not *American Idol* caliber, although we believed we were, at the time. Sorry to say, we didn't get selected! I wondered years later what sort of parents would allow their 10-year-old girls to sing a song like that. Ours did!

As we got a little older, we giggled about the boys we had crushes on. We also shaved all the hair off our arms and legs together. That's right, even our arms. We didn't know it would come back! I'm not sure which of us suggested that one, but I can tell you, it was *NOT* fun suffering through the regrowth.

One of the things I remember most about our friendship is the pledge we made to each other to prove our allegiance. We pricked our fingers, touched them together and swore (not cursed) we would always be Best Friends. A few days later, Nancy and a couple other neighborhood kids 'egged' our house. So much for our BFF oath. I guess she must have been *mad at me* for something. One of the *only* good things I've discovered thus far about getting older is, you can't always remember who is *mad at you*, or why! I believe that's a good thing. Ha!

When I was 13 years old, Nancy was there for me when my Dad passed away suddenly. She sat next to me at the funeral home, and even though she didn't say a word, I could see she was almost as sad as I was. The following year, I had to change schools. We vowed again, nothing or no one would ever come between our friendship. Unfortunately, as life would have it, we both made new friends and slowly drifted apart. Time, and now miles, have separated us even more. Once in a while when I return *home,* we still get together for tea, and pick up right where we left off.

When my Mother passed away a few years ago, and I went back to Erie, Nancy was the first person to show up at our door with a meal for my family. It was the same house where we played all those years ago. As we walked up and down the familiar streets, we spoke of each friend as we passed their house, and wondered how they were doing. We had a history. We were family. I'm sure even IF I called Nancy today, she would still be available for me, as I would be for her. Thank you Nancy for being my very first Forever Friend.

So, What's a Girl to DO?

Who are the GirlFriends who come to mind when you read this? It doesn't need to be someone from long ago. Why not put this book down and give her a call. Personally thank her for being a Forever Friend who impacted your life in such a way, which lasts for a lifetime. You may not want to call her now if it's late into the night. Although, if you do, when she sees it's you, being the kind of a GirlFriend she is, she'll probably pick up the phone after the very first ring!

Count your blessings by making a list of all your Forever Friends, past and present. What characteristics make a Forever Friend for you?

_____

_____

FAITHFUL FRIEND

She is the one you reach out to when you need sound counsel. She may be your Forever Friend, but not always. You know she'll give you good advice, not just tell you what you want to hear. Your Faithful Friend may be your equal or even a few steps further along in her spiritual walk. This relationship *could* also be a one-sided friendship, as in a mentor, life coach, or small group leader at church. She doesn't let you stay stuck in a situation too long before reminding you of who you are, and *Whose* you are. She motivates you to be better, without making you feel like there's something wrong with you.

She inspires you with her words, and by the way she lives her life, which all line up. Your Faithful Friend has deep wisdom, who not only knows God's Words but teaches you how to apply it to your everyday situations. This spiritual friend may not be interested in going shopping or spending the day at the beach, but IF *you* asked her to, she would probably go ~ for *YOU*!

One of my favorite books, *Balcony People*, by Joyce Landorf, has always challenged me to live in such a way as to be that kind of positive influence in my GirlFriends lives. Do I always succeed? No, but I don't give up trying. The author explains this type of friendship by saying "There are those who are on the *balcony* of our life, lifting us up, cheering us on, and energizing us with their affirmations and encouragement. There are other girls we all know, who do exactly the opposite, as they drag us down with their negativity and *conditional* love." Obviously, these are the *Basement People*. We will be examining a couple of those girls later in this chapter.

This pretty little velvet-covered book was given to me by Rita, a one time Fringe Friend of mine. Interestingly, she was my boss in a decorating company we both worked for. After I became a manager, we transitioned into Faithful Friends. I am blessed to say that even now, after almost 40 years, we have remained Forever Friends to one another. The progression from Fringe to Faithful, to Forever, came after pouring large amounts of time and attention into each other's lives. Enduring friendships are typically not a sprint, but rather they are more like a marathon!

So, What's a Girl to DO?

Write down those GirlFriends who have been your *Balcony* or Faithful Friends? If you don't have one, be intentional about finding one. Ask God to bring her into your life or look around because she might already be there. Who could you be a Balcony GirlFriend to?

FORMER FRIEND

This Friend may not necessarily be what you are thinking, although she could be. These girls are not always Frenemies: they can simply be Former Friends. They may have been wonderful GirlFriends you were very close with, at one time. There are many reasons which cause us to lose a friendship, and it may not always be bad. Perhaps you were college roommates, worked together for years, or were in each other's weddings. What *do* you do with all those bridesmaids' dresses anyway?

A variety of circumstances like time, distance, priorities, and life changes can cause us to grow apart. It happens. Close friendships may wane because we have less in common with each other than we did at one time, thus desiring little interest to hang out together. I call these Fading Friends. It's ok, it's all in the natural course of life and friendships.

Can you imagine what our lives would be like if we kept ALL the GirlFriends we acquired from nursery school until now, never having said good-bye to any of them? It would be totally impossible to fit everyone and everything into our already busy lives and hectic schedules, and still keep our sanity! Even though we might miss many of our Former Friends, we can always remember our good times together with great affection.

Obviously, there's a flip side to Former Friends being a positive thing. We typically *break ties* with a GirlFriend because of unresolved conflicts. Maybe you can't see eye to eye on key issues. Betrayal, Gossip, Jealousy, and all the other *Games* we'll discuss in the upcoming chapters can lead us to having '*unfriendly endings*'! It could also happen if one of you did something hurtful but refused to apologize. Ever had a situation like that?

When there is a difference between how much 'space' you need in a friendship, and how much the other girl wants, a friendship could also dissolve. Other times, there may be unrealistic or unspoken expectations placed on you which you couldn't meet. If those expectations are unknown, not agreed to, it can be very difficult, if not impossible, to maintain a friendship without some underlying residue. We'll cover this topic in greater depth later in the book.

So, What's a Girl to DO?

Which of your Former Friends do you miss the most, good or bad? What was the gift they forever implanted in your life? Today *could* be a good day to reconnect with her.

FRINGE FRIEND

These are the Girl Friends who know the facts about each other. She may be aware of where you work, if you're married or single, and possibly what you do for fun. Did you notice I separated the word GirlFriends? It symbolizes that you are not in a close relationship with these girls. You are more 'friendly' rather than' friends'.

These friendships are more of an exchange of pleasantries. "Hi, How's it going," etc. You seldom, if ever, get into the deeper things of life. She could work at your bank, live in your neighborhood or be your Dental Hygienist, which makes it rather difficult to have a two-way conversation when someone is poking around your gums or picking the poppy seeds out from between your teeth! My apologies to all Hygienists. It's not personal, please don't be mad at me!

Perhaps the Fringe is a Friend of one of your GirlFriends. The majority of your time with them is spent in groups, or participating in social activities together. Your kids may attend the same school, or you may be in a *spin* class together, so these activities are what most conversations center around. We all have people we exchange small talk and facts with each day, and these types of relationships can still be very beneficial.

But, what if you wanted to turn a casual acquaintance into a Faithful or Forever Friend, as I did with Rita? Go ahead, make room for God to bring a new friend into your life or deepen an already existing one. Perhaps it will be an unexpected blessing to the both of you.

This was my experience during a time when I was terribly hurt and betrayed by some people. Annette was a girl I casually knew from church; I would have called her a Fringe Friend. She randomly showed up at my house one day with a large bouquet of hydrangeas, my all time favorite flowers. Strangely enough, she didn't know that at the time.

I assumed she had heard about my situation, so I proceeded to ask who told her, since I had only shared it with a couple of my Faithful Friends. She said no one told her anything, except God. She said, "God just told me to buy these flowers and bring them to YOU!"

After I burst into tears, she gently 'pushed' herself through my front door and into my life, as I slowly and carefully shared some of the deepest wounds of my heart with her. She listened to God, even when she didn't know the reason she was coming to my house! That's all He wanted of her, and each of us ~ is to be available to *GO* and be a blessing to someone, and let Him do the rest. It's what *walking by faith and not by sight* means in a practical way.

At a time when I needed Him most, He was expressing to me, through her, I was not forgotten, that He knew me personally (my FAVORITE flowers), and that He loved me! From that point on, the process of us becoming Forever Friends began! Thank you, Annette, for being obedient, and for showing me God's love.

So, What's a Girl to DO?

Can you recall a time when a friend went from a Fringe to a Forever Friend? Who might you consider taking to the next level? IF you can trust her with your story, why not take the risk!

Looking over each kind of GirlFriends we've covered so far, what kind of friend are You? What are the qualities above you want to improve on? What can you intentionally do to nourish a friendship this week, and with whom?

I'm trusting each of these GirlFriends brought a smile to your face, as you took note of how each affected your life in a positive way. That certainly does *NOT* mean you didn't have your share of struggles in your relationship. You may have even been *mad* at each other from time to time. Most of us aren't expecting *Perfection* in our Friendships, we are all simply desiring *Connection*.

One day I asked my then 7 year old niece, Alayna, why Katherine was her very best friend. She quickly replied: *"Because she understands me."* I am not sure what there is to *figure out* about a 7 year old, but isn't that what we all want in a GirlFriend? Our former pastor, Dr. Percy Augustine, often said it this way. *"The greatest need of the human heart is to be understood."* I guess Alayna figured out the importance of that pretty early on in life. Do you have a GirlFriend who honestly understands you? I sure hope so. Would your GirlFriends say you truly understand and accept them?

Now, in fairytales, all friendships would be rewarding and supportive like those we just covered, and that would be very *GOOD*. However, we all know that it's just not always the way it is in the 'real' world. Now, that is *BAD* (and *SAD*). We disagree, we misunderstand, get jealous, bossy, competitive, and sometimes we even get *MAD*!

Navigating through the difficult times we experience with GirlFriends reminds me of a story I heard recently of how palm trees survive in hurricane winds. I learned that the tree can bend all the way down to the ground and yet not break. *IF* the tree is healthy, in time, it will bounce straight back up. What happens is, right in the middle of a storm, it's roots will dig deeper into the ground to make it stronger than it was before the storm.

Something you think would destroy it, does exactly the opposite. It might not look like a good situation from the outside, but it's only because we are unaware of what's really taking place below the surface. It's not that the palm tree *resists* the winds, rather it adjusts and adapts to them.

I believe this can be compared to our friendships. When both GirlFriends are healthy and 'rooted' in Jesus and His Word, the 'winds' of conflict will not destroy it. Just as with the palm tree, not only will it survive the stress put on it, but *IF* we *adapt* and *adjust* our thoughts and attitudes towards one another, it can actually make for an even stronger relationship. Going through these pressures will reveal to us our true *root system*. Where does your strength come from?

It's important we know God's remedies for dealing with these types of *storms* in our lives, and be equipped to respond to them *before* the winds begin howling around us. Here in Florida, we call this Hurricane Preparedness. Are you ready to handle the possible turbulence in your friendships?

Which brings me to the last 2 types of Girl Friends we need to be prepared to *withstand*. As I stated at the beginning of this chapter, it is God who allows each girl to enter our lives, to teach us something. Yes, we can even learn from these Fake and Fatal girls. Hopefully, they won't hang around any longer than necessary, so, learn your lessons quickly, GirlFriends! After you hear about them, I believe we will all agree they probably are *NOT* your friends at all. Having said that, let's cautiously proceed to the darker side of friendships.

FAKE FRIEND

IF you characterize these ladies by their actions, you will never be fooled by their words, which will prove to be the opposite. Proverbs 26:23-25 says, "Smooth words may hide a wicked heart, just as a pretty glaze covers a clay pot. People may cover their hatred with pleasant words, but they're deceiving you. They pretend to be kind, but don't believe them. Their hearts are full of many evils." Yowzer!

One of the most glaring signs of this Fake Friend is she usually only calls you when she needs something. Of course, there's nothing wrong with doing a friend a favor, that's what GirlFriends do. But, when it happens on a consistent basis, and she is not willing to return a favor, she is probably a 'user' disguised as a GirlFriend. She is extremely self-centered and seldom, if ever, asks what *you* want to do or what is going on in your life (don't tell her). Remember, a true GirlFriend will focus on what she can *give* to a friendship, not only on what she can *get* from it!

If you have a crisis, this girl is missing in action. One of the hallmark characteristics of a Fake Friend is that she doesn't think twice about saying negative or hurtful things *to* you or *about* you. This is a girl who usually tries to discourage you or hold you back when you want to pursue new things, or other GirlFriends.

IF you have a prestigious role at work, church, or in the community, these Fake Friends will probably be the first to *volunteer* to help you. But, watch out for 'Suzie the status seeker', she typically wants only one thing. She wants to be seen as important, and that's accomplished by being seen with you.

She's always looking for new ways to climb the social, corporate or any other ladder, no matter what method she needs to use to get there. She believes the end justifies her means. This kind of girl can easily turn into our next category of Fatal Friend, *IF* you allow her to.

I have a Forever Friend, whom I love dearly. She is kind, funny, generous, loving and forgiving, and would do *ANYTHING* for you, to a fault. Her fault! I will change her name to 'Mary', so she doesn't get *mad* at me. (Like she can't figure out it's her) She is so nice, that certain types of Fake Friends will gravitate toward her and try to take advantage of her, because of her sincere desire to help others. Now, that really makes me *mad*!

I humbly say to you, my sweet GirlFriends, if you have this same pattern of being a rescuer, to paraphrase an old proverb: The first time they *use* you, shame on them. The second time they take advantage of you, shame on them. The third time I'm sorry to say, but shame on *you*! You are the *daughter of the Most High God*, and there is absolutely no reason for you to let another person treat you in such a disrespectful manner.

I think as Christian women, we sometimes take the admonition to *Love One Another* to an unhealthy, unbalanced place. It's called being codependent. I can't tell you when that takes place, only God can do that. However, my suggestion would be to ask Him to give you wisdom to know who needs you to help them, who should learn to help themselves, and who must go directly to Jesus to provide what they need. I can honestly say, it's not always going to be by going through you.

Practice setting clear-cut boundaries with this girl. Once you set them though, they need to be non-negotiable. *IF* she accepts them, it will help provide stability to a controlling or Fake Friendship. Don't let her 'shame and blame' you into changing them either, especially if you believe they are the right ones for you. One of the best books I've ever read on this subject is *Boundaries,* by Dr. Henry Cloud and Dr. John Townsend.

A little pop quiz to test yourself with this type of friendship:

Can I be myself around her?

Can I trust her or do I need to be careful with what I say?

Does she show an interest in what's going on in my life?

Do I feel better after spending time with her?

Does she accept me for who I am?

Does she put unrealistic expectations or rules on me?

Your honest answers will tell you if this girl is a true friend or an imposter.

I am thrilled to tell you 'Mary' *is* gaining much wisdom and insight into setting healthy boundaries, and learning who she should or should not permit into her close circle of Friends. Remember, when you say "Yes" to allowing one person in your life, it means you're saying "No" to someone else God may have intended for you. 'Mary' now has more time to spend with her family, her ministry, and her real GirlFriends ~ Like *ME*!

So, What's a Girl to DO?

Are you bombarded by Fake Friends who constantly take up needless time and energy? Who are they? What are specific steps you will take to handle these types of relationships?

Last, and definitely the *least* type of girl we should be involved with is the:

FATAL Friend!

Just as her name expresses, she is a deadly one! She is the exact opposite of your Forever Friend, who speaks life into you. This girl is toxic to you in every way. She can literally make you sick: physically, emotionally, mentally, and even spiritually. She increases your vulnerability to all the stress related symptoms like higher blood pressure, a lower immune system, high anxiety, depression, and the list continues. She drains the life right out of you with her negativism, gossip, put downs, competition, and complaining.

She constantly goes over the same tedious list of all the bad things that have ever happened to her in her life. She may even get *mad* at you if she thinks you are not giving her enough attention or sympathy. Heaven forbid, you should look away or roll your eyes during one of her ongoing 'recitations'!

In order to make up for her insecurities, she must attempt to make you feel bad about yourself, so she can build up herself in her own eyes. She will even *throw you under the bus* with your other GirlFriends, if it makes her look better. Rather than rejoicing with you, this *prophet of gloom* will try to make you feel guilty for the blessings you have.

She may not even be aware that her behavior is making you feel 'trapped like a rat', but look out for her cunningness, and don't take the bait. 1 Peter 5:8 tells us to "Be alert and sober minded. Our enemy prowls around like a roaring lion looking for someone to devour." That is exactly what this girl will do. She will *eat your lunch.* Or should I say, she will eat *YOU* for lunch, then spit you out! YUK! This is how this character will make you feel after spending any amount of time with her. One of her favorite lines she likes to use on you and others is, "*Oh, and you call yourself such a good Christian.*" Have you ever heard that one?

When you begin to feel you *need* to stay in this type of relationship more than you *want* to, it's time to say goodbye gracefully. She might not be a bad person at heart, but she is definitely not good for your heart! Proverbs 4:23 even warns us to "Guard your heart." If you have tried to bring some of her ungodly habits to her attention, but she either doesn't change, or says she will, but never does, it's time to let her go. Slowly stop spending time with her or let her know, it's just not working for you anymore.

I want to be clear here. We are not talking about a *real* GirlFriend who occasionally has a bad day or is going through a difficult period in her life. We have all experienced that. More than ever, we need our GirlFriend's support during those times. This is a girl who is consistent with this type of toxic behavior. I hope you don't have any Fatal Friends in your circle, but *IF* you do, I pray you would be willing to remove yourself from the situation, in a humble and gentle manner.

So, What's a Girl to DO?

Who is that Fatal friend in your life? What are the necessary steps you will take to 'unfriend' her?

I don't know about you, but I am totally drained by simply describing this dangerous girl. I'm going to take a little nap right now and will be back shortly. I suggest you do the same!

Ok, I feel refreshed, how about you? See what happens when we focus on the negative...hmmm.

Speaking of 'unfriending' someone. Social media has greatly changed the definition of a friend in recent years. With the click of a button or a tap on the screen, we can catch up with old friends, make new connections, block someone who has offended us or 'unfriend' those we have lost interest in. But having a thousand online 'is still no substitute for having a few close friends you spend time with face to face.

There was a survey done recently, which extensively examined data collected from heavy social internet users. The results showed the majority of people questioned indicated they felt lonelier and more isolated now than they did before *connecting* online. Internet 'friends' can't give you a hug when you need one, bring you soup when you're sick or celebrate all the joys in your life *with* you. Emojis certainly can be cute, but they typically don't cut it as a substitute for being present with a GirlFriend.

Please don't be *mad* at me for saying this, but I would encourage you to spend most of your time investing in the *real* world with your *real* Girlfriends, opposed to using up huge amounts of time with online relationships, *IF* possible. There, I said it!

Well, enough said about this ~ for now. We'll discuss this topic more in depth in a later chapter. I'm sure you can't wait!

Now that we have completed Part I of *GirlFriends Rule*, let's get ready to be challenged in Part II, in the *Rule Breakers* section. As we move ahead, we will deal with several 'fouls' which take place while playing *Games* with our GirlFriends. Aren't you happy I suggested taking a nap? Now, to wake yourself up for what's ahead, grab yourself a cup of coffee or your drink of choice. Hebrews 12:1 advises us to "Throw off every weight that hinders us, and the sins which so easily entangle us". Why? So we can "run with endurance the race God has set before us."

Are we ready for this? Then, Let the *Games* Begin!

PART II

*** *Rule Breakers* ***

If Your GirlFriend is

Gossiping to You About

Someone Else,

She is Probably

Gossiping to Someone Else

About You!

CHAPTER 3
Well, Bless Her Heart!

"Gossip is spread by wicked people, it stirs up trouble and separates close friends."

Proverbs 16:28

Wicked people! Those are some pretty strong words for simply passing on information about someone, isn't it? I think most of us honestly enjoy hearing a juicy little story now and then, unless of course, that story is about you! Let's face it, there are some people who thrive on *stirring the pot*. We even have entire tv channels, news publications, and magazines which get paid to *dig up dirt* on others.

It doesn't really matter if their *reporting* contains even a morsel of truth or not. Who reads and listens to these things anyway? I hope not you. So, is Gossip really all that big a deal? Let's *dig around* a bit ourselves to uncover what the facts versus fiction are concerning Gossip.

We'll begin with that oh, so subtle statement of, *"Well, Bless Her Heart."* First, a special note to all my Southern GirlFriends, and I have many of you living here in Florida. Please, don't be *mad* at me for what I'm about to say to you. When using this endearing phrase, I am certain most of the time y'all come from a very sincere place, especially when a GirlFriend is struggling.

Here comes the *but*. But I also know, on occasion, these words have been used at the end of an insult, as though adding them somehow miraculously offsets your hurtful, demeaning, or judgmental words. *OUCH*! Let me give you an example of what I overheard recently when two girls were discussing a mutual friend. *"Oh my, I wonder who picked out Amy's outfit today. It's way too short and tight for her odd body shape. She really needs a stylist. Well, Bless her heart!"* Understood? Good, keep reading because I'm not done.

Next, to my Northern, Eastern, Western, and everyone in between GirlFriends. I am *NOT* letting the rest of us off the hook that easily. It's the same *Game* we play, we just use different words. How about something like *"Did you hear what Nicole did, don't tell anyone I told you, but ..."* Or *"Well, we really need to pray for Tracy, I just heard she ..."* This not so nice *Game* we're playing is the good old-fashioned *Gossip Game*, and it's no fun, especially when it's at your expense!

There is nothing that can harm a relationship more than a GirlFriend spreading rumors, lies, and even unflattering personal truths concerning another. The damage done to people's feelings, reputations, friendships, and lives by Gossiping can be irreversible. As stated in our *Focus Verse*, Gossip definitely *can*, and *does*, part even the best of friends. I'm sure you or someone you know, has been forever impacted by these types of careless words spoken.

DEFINITION of GOSSIP:

Webster describes it as: *A conversation concerning the personal details of another person's life, sometimes with a malicious intent, but not always. The New Testament Greek word means whisperer, talebearer, or idle talker.*

A Gossiper then is a person who whispers something about another, usually behind her back. The bible links Slander and Gossip together and calls them *sister sins*. Surely not the kind of *sister* I want to have. Do you? In Romans 1:29-31, Paul lists the many sins of a depraved mind. Guess which ones were included, right in the middle along with murderers and haters of God. You got it: Gossip and Slander! The difference between the two is:

Slander is usually a calculated, false, unsupported, or malicious statement which intends to injure a person's reputation.

Gossip on the other hand, doesn't always start with a deliberate attempt to harm someone; it's typically to pass on someone else's information. However, it can quickly and easily escalate to criticism or defaming of the person. It is more of an idle talk about a person's character or private information, typically to put them down and elevate yourself.

Most of us, if we were honest, would admit we've been on both sides of the Gossip aisle before. You may be thinking, 'Oh, come on now, I was just stating the facts.' That might be the case, but the facts and the truth still hurt other people, especially when they are not there to defend themselves. Besides, sometimes it's just your opinion or someone else's version of the truth. You know the way it is, GirlFriends. There's your truth, their truth, then the whole truth, so help you God! Either way, Gossip is not lady-like, not Christ-like, and most importantly, it's just plain wrong. Remember, it's not me who says that ~ it's God.

So, is it ever okay to talk about someone else when they're not there? The answer to that question is a resounding, "*YES.*" Whew! It's perfectly fine to deliver good news you heard about a GirlFriend, as long as it's public knowledge or you have her permission to. What do you think the distinction is? The real difference between passing on legitimate information and Gossip, is your *motive*. What is your intention?

The true heart test is found in Ephesians. 4:29, where we read: "Let no corrupt communication proceed out of your mouth, but ONLY what is good for edification (to build her up), that it may give grace to the hearers." That's it. Like all our parents so wisely told us at one time or another: *"If you can't say something nice about someone..."* you finish the sentence...That's right ... *"Then, don't say anything at all!"*

Do you have GirlFriends who frequently *dish out* Gossip about others? Perhaps it's you who is a Gossip Addict. Telling stories about your GirlFriends, sometimes flattering, but other times, not so much. Anyone who's ever tried to stop herself from Gossiping, usually finds it's not as easy a habit to kick, as you might have thought. You are not alone, though. A research team at the University of Amsterdam found recently a whopping 90 percent of total office conversations qualify as Gossip. Now, that could make you very afraid to leave the room!

In the event you didn't already *hear about this one*: Celebrity Gossip is a more than $3 billion industry. That's right, *BILLION*! Even though Gossip is a harmful habit, some people seem to find it to be fun, while they are involved in it. However, talking about others often leaves them feeling regretful after they've let the *cat out of the bag!*

I saw a pillow recently which read: 'I don't repeat gossip, so listen carefully the first time.' I realize that is a cute and funny saying, but I also know Gossip is not a laughing matter. If you have difficulty holding your tongue, and want to change your Gossip routine, you must begin by taking an honest look at what you are *getting out* of it. In other words, what's the payoff?

If we know it hurts our GirlFriends, then why do we continue to take part in this *Game*? One of the main reasons we Gossip is because we typically don't feel good about ourselves. Let's take a look now at some of the other underlying causes of why we are such willing participants, knowing God's Word warns us against it.

Here is a little Gossip test for you to take. You may rate yourself on this one.

Are you trying to make yourself appear better in someone else's eyes or even your own, when talking about a GirlFriend? YOU would never do that, right?

Do you feel excited or can't wait to tell someone else's story, before she does or anyone else?

Does it make you feel important when you have insider information your other GirlFriends don't have?

Would you make these same comments IF your GirlFriend were standing in front of you? If your answer is Yes, how do you believe your words would make her feel?

Have you noticed others may not be gossiping to you, or not confiding as often as they used to? Is it possible you have developed a reputation of being untrustworthy?

When there is a lull in a conversation, do you talk about other GirlFriends, who are not there, as a way of filling in the gaps?

Does it make you feel special when you are the center of attention while you are sharing your 'news'?

Does it give you a temporary boost, but afterwards you feel worse?

Do you notice people cringing when you are 'sharing'?

Do you often begin a sentence with "I need to tell you something, but you need to promise not to tell anyone else?" That's when you need to STOP yourself!

Did any of your answers make you feel *uncomfortable*? To sum it up, GirlFriends, we Gossip for a variety of reasons. Put a check next to those which are true for you.

1. Makes you feel superior.

2. Want to be a part of the group.

3. Are bored with the conversation.

4. Want revenge for being hurt.

5. Enjoy the attention.

6. Jealous of your GirlFriend.

7. Simply unhappy with yourself.

Being on the receiving end of Gossip was the primary reason I wrote this book. I never had a desire to become a writer, but because my experience regarding Gossip was so hurtful to me and damaging to others, I felt the need to share some of my findings with you. My hope is that out of my pain, I can encourage and warn you to stay far from the temptation to be involved in this hurtful habit.

I thought it was so sweet, yet profound, what my 13-year-old grandson, Alex, said to me this week. While were talking about some friends, in a good way of course, who were going through a difficult time, he said: "*Well, you know Gramma, without challenges, you can't build character!"* Thank you for that great reminder, *'Pastor'* Alex!

God's Word says it like this: "He comes alongside us when we go through hard times, and before you know it, He brings us alongside someone else who is going through hard times so that we can be there for that person just as God was there for us." 2 Corinthians 1:4-6

So, Here is My Character Building Story ~

Several years ago, I was made aware of two friends who were not on speaking terms. At one time, they were inseparable. They were both leaders in the church, and I considered them both my GirlFriends. So, being a peacemaker, and a pastor's wife, I felt it was my responsibility to see if I could be a mediator. You know, help them reconcile. I spoke with each separately, and to my delight, they agreed to meet.

We met on a Sunday afternoon, and made every attempt to get to the core of their misunderstanding. After several hours of hashing things out, each one stating their case as they saw it, they finally came to an agreement. They simply agreed to disagree. Neither viewed the situation that happened in quite the same way. These are the times we need to decide *IF* we want to prove we are right more than we want to extend grace and peace to our GirlFriends. Because they valued their relationship *more*, they chose to move forward as friends, nonetheless.

Mission accomplished. Whew, glad that was over, or was it?

I then made the terrible mistake of saying to them: "*We are all friends, so as long as we are already here, is there anything else you would like to get off your chests?*" Of course, by now you probably have guessed what happened next and I only wish I would have. One of the girls said: "*YES, there is.*" She looked in my direction and proceeded to say the following words: "*Friends, what do you mean friends? We are not friends; I don't like you, and I don't trust you either!*"

Obviously, I turned around to see who *must* have entered the room behind me. To my dismay, there was no one else there. Just me. She was looking straight at me, and talking to *ME*, about *ME*. It sent such shockwaves throughout my entire body, that even writing these words after all these years have passed, still makes me tremble. It's in moments like these, when the pressures of life squeeze you, the *real you* will come out!

Now, this is a girl I had never had any disagreements with, as far as I was aware. I thought of her as a Fringe Friend, yet now I find out she basically *HATES* my guts. I wanted to shout, 'Are you kidding me, I just spent my entire Sunday afternoon helping you, and THIS is what I get? After all I've done for you. How could you not like me ~ everyone else does?' It's amazing how fast your mind can talk to you in such a short period of time! Not that I would ever say any of those things out loud, of course.

While trying to absorb these devastating words, all I could do was stare down at the table and *PRAY*. Not knowing what to say next, I noticed what the bracelet I was wearing said, 'What would Jesus do?' Great timing God! Even though I really didn't *feel* like following His direction, I made the choice not to react to all the negative voices in my head. Instead, I decided to respond the way He would want me to.

I said to myself, 'Self, James 1:19 says we are to be "Slow to speak, Slow to anger, and Quick to listen." I was so traumatized at the time that I began to wonder if it said to be, Quick to speak, Quick to answer, and Slow to listen! That didn't sound quite right, so I calmly forced out the words: "*Really? I'm so sorry you feel that way. Did I do or say something to offend you?"* Trust me when I tell you, this is what we would call a modern-day miracle. She said *"No, you didn't hurt me personally, but"* then she proceeded to explain how a mutual, unnamed friend, told her I had Gossiped about someone while at a women's meeting in my home.

With my next response, I fought hard, I mean *really* hard, not to say, 'Give me that girl's name and number, I'm going to set her straight.' I prayed again for the strength not to be defensive. I simply informed her, not only did I not speak those words, but I was totally unaware of the situation she had just enlightened me of. Hmm, so who was the real *reporter* here? I'm just kidding.

For further clarification, I did ask her who the person was who was kind enough to *share* that with her, instead of me. She wouldn't name the tale bearer, because she didn't want to break her confidence. I understood that, sort of. Unfortunately, the problem was that I had now become the girl who was stuck with this 'guilty, until proven innocent' label. I would now be left with the task of looking among my other GirlFriends, wondering which of my them was the *whisperer.* That's part of the mess we are left to clean up after Gossip has done it's damage.

Our other friend, who was still sitting there taking this all in, you know the one she was 'originally' *mad* at, finally spoke up. She announced she had also attended that same meeting, and never heard me say anything to that effect. Of course I didn't. Had I said it, I would have fessed up. It would not have been the first time I had messed up, but this was not one of those times. Unfortunately, she had also become trapped in this *Game,* feeling an uncomfortable need to pick sides.

Another byproduct of Gossip are the poisonous tentacles which reach far beyond the GirlFriends originally involved. Other women who heard, and possibly believed the *informant's* version of the story, began asking on Facebook why we were all *mad* at each other. I simply responded to those who were curious enough to ask me by saying: *"I am not mad at anyone."*

I tried to quickly stomp out the *fire* while it was still a spark. Sadly, it doesn't usually work that way. The rumors continued to spread like wildfire, and unfortunately, *burned* many women for years to come. "Without wood, the fire goes out. Without Gossip, contention stops." Proverbs 26:20

I eventually found out who the *whisperer* was, and realized it was more of a statement about her. As deeply as that situation hurt me, I made the difficult decision to let it go, and not confront her. Instead, I let my reputation speak for itself, and reminded myself of the truth that those who knew me still loved and trusted me.

I'm unsure why this girl, who I barely knew, felt the need to spread her misunderstood story to others instead of coming directly to me. Sometimes people already have their minds made up about you, and for whatever reason, nothing you say or do will convince them otherwise.

God's remedy for Gossip are the specific principles He set down in His Word, which give us wisdom on how to act, but not react. However, I can guarantee you, your mind will probably still fight you all the way, as mine did. Had I not *hidden* those verses in my heart, I would have been left with only my own defensive thoughts and bruised feelings, and we saw which direction that was heading!

Remember, just because something is said about you or anyone else, doesn't mean it's true! Instead of rushing out to defend yourself to everyone, we can ask God to be our Defender, and consider these alternative responses to handling Gossip. "The Lord is my mighty Defender, perfect and just in all His ways. Our God is faithful and true. He does what is right and fair." Deuteronomy 32:4.

So, What's a Girl to DO, IF Someone Gossips about YOU?

---

*Go to the source. If the rumor or facts are about you, and it's harmful, try to find out who started it. Approach her in a humble, non-aggressive way, of course.

*Allow yourself time to grieve. Whether the information is true or not, it's normal to feel hurt or betrayed.

*Pray for conviction and repentance for her. Since we can't control what others say or do, there's no way to prevent others from talking about us.

*Return a blessing for a curse. Don't Gossip to others about her Gossiping about you!

*Let your reputation speak for itself. Establish credibility by living like Jesus calls us to. Have confidence in who you really are. Your GirlFriends know and love you.

*Overlook Gossip when and *IF* you can. You can't run around putting out Gossip fires all the time. Can you think of a time when you were affected by Gossip? How was it resolved?

We must learn to think before we speak, and choose our words carefully to build up one another, rather than tear our GirlFriends down. Before we are tempted to Gossip, let's ask ourselves these questions, I heard attributed to Bernard Meltzer.

So, What's a Girl to DO, If YOU are the Gossiper?

- **Is it true**? Did you see or hear it for yourself, or was it second-hand information?

- **Is it kind?** How would you feel if she made those types of statements about you?

- **Is it fair?** Does it build up a GirlFriend or tear her down?

- **Is it necessary?** Does it make your relationship better?

First, and foremost, we must confess our sin to God and ask Him to forgive us. Whether we want to admit it or not, Gossip is a sin, and it breaks our communication with Him. We need to ask Him to help us keep our tongue from Gossiping. You will need to ask your GirlFriend to forgive you also. That's a tough one, I know. But, if you don't admit it to her, it will hinder your relationship in much the way it does between you and God. Whether you realize it or not, it will build a wall between the two of you, even if she never knows you talked about her.

One day you will wonder why the two of you are not as close as you once were. Could Gossip be the reason? It's scary, but it's also very healing, and the only way to have an authentic relationship. You will then be able to look your GirlFriend in the eye, with a clear conscience, and know there is nothing you will ever say about her again that would hurt her if she heard it. James

5:16 says we are to "Confess your sins to one another, that you may be healed."

Be honest and ask yourself the reason/reasons YOU Gossip?

Summing up Exhortations for the Gossiper:

1. Just DON'T do it! Refuse to play this *Game*.

2. Ask God's forgiveness.

3. Be honest with yourself concerning your Gossip habit, and why you do it.

4. Begin with a ONE day a week *Gossip Fast*! Reread it, Not *FEAST*. Practice it.

5. Ask forgiveness of your GirlFriends you Gossiped *to*, and *about*.

6. Stop immediately and apologize when you catch yourself Gossiping.

7. Get a trusted GirlFriend to hold you accountable.

Resist the urge to Gossip or even speak the truth, if your motives are not pure. "She who guards her mouth, protects her life, but she who opens her lips invites her own ruin!" Proverbs 13:3. The way I see it is, every time a GirlFriend Gossips, there are a minimum of three people who have been affected. We talked about the Gossiper and the person being Gossiped about. However, what if you are an innocent bystander, and witness Gossip going on around you? That, my friend is quite the quandary to be in.

It puts you right in the middle of trying to figure out who is telling the truth, and forces you to choose between GirlFriends. How unfair is that? We typically have four choices when confronted with hearing Gossip. There may be different responses for each individual circumstance. So, you will need to determine what avenue to pursue, depending on the situation.

1. All too often, we tend to join in on the negative conversation. This would be your worst choice, for obvious reasons.

2. You might listen to what is being said and say nothing. This is almost the same as agreeing with the Gossiper! Why would you choose this option? To protect yourself?

3. You could simply walk away. But, be warned, *IF* you choose this alternative, *YOU* risk being the subject of her next Gossip session. Is it worth the risk?

4. Be bold and take a stand, by standing up for your GirlFriend! I will admit, this can be intimidating. However, if you choose this response you'll want to take the 'high road', by being careful not to put yourself *above* the Gossiper.

If you decide to go with the latter and want to respond to the *tattletale*, one of the best questions psychologists say you can ask someone who is trying to involve you in Gossip, is: *"Why are you telling me this?"* The girl who is initiating the conversation, might be caught off guard by your question, because most of the time, they are not accustomed to being *called out*. Usually, they will not have a good excuse for why they are saying what they are, or for including you in their conversation.

She is probably telling you simply because you're there! This question will force her to face the fact you are not going to be a willing participant in this Gossip *Game*. Even if what is being said is true, your response should always be to defend your GirlFriend being talked about in the best possible way. GirlFriends protect their GirlFriends, which includes their reputations. Isn't that what you would want her to do for you?

You could also say something like:

a. "I know so and so, and that does not sound like her to me."

b. "I am feeling uncomfortable, so perhaps we could talk about something else."

c. "I have been working on not talking about people who are not present."

d. "Maybe you could speak to her personally about this issue."

e. Praise the positive characteristics of your GirlFriend who is being talked about.

Make a decision, once and for all, not to partake in Gossip. Remember, if a GirlFriend is Gossiping about someone when she is with you, she is probably Gossiping about *you* when she is with someone else! Think about that one! "Life and death are in the power of the tongue", so let's choose life, GirlFriends! Proverbs 18:21

Just Because

You are Offended

By a GirlFriend,

Doesn't Mean

You are Right!

CHAPTER 4
She Makes Me Sooo Mad!

"A friend Offended is harder to win back than a strong city."

Proverbs 18:19

In the *good ole days*, there used to be only a few ways to play this Offense *Game*. You either experienced a face to face exchange, a conversation on the home phone, which was attached to the wall, a *Dear Jane* letter or you simply heard through the *grapevine* your GirlFriend was mad at you.

With the electronic age of social media being a way of life today, the means to Offend or be Offended, have escalated to catastrophic proportions. We can in the blink of an eye, a tap on a screen, or click of a mouse, be insulted or Offended by someone on Instagram, Facebook, Twitter or YouTube ~ just to name a few. It can also take place via Instant Messages, Tweets, Texts, Emails or through whatever new media is in vogue in the future. Well, you get the message!

Matthew 24:10 tells us, "In the last days, many will be Offended, and they will hate one another." I believe this to be more true today than at any other time in our country's history. I think it's quite interesting that the Greek definition of the word Offense is 'skandalon'. It's the area of a trap where the bait is attached. Its job is simply to lure in the animal.

When you are Offended by someone, remember it is Satan's way of setting a trap for *you*. The end payoff, *IF* we choose to take the bait, is for us to become bitter, resentful, and unforgiving towards the Offender. But beware, because *YOU* are the one who will get caught in that trap, not the person you're setting it for.

Another way to explain the results of holding onto Offenses is the adage of it's like 'You drinking the poison, but waiting for the other person to die.' Holding onto grudges or *drinking in* an Offense, can slowly eat away at us, sometimes even causing us to become physically ill. In this chapter, we'll learn how to Defuse the Offense and Refuse the temptation to drink from that *cup*. So, what is the definition of an Offense?

DEFINITION of OFFENSE:

Thesaurus.com says: *To cause a person to feel hurt, pain, anger or to be upset by what another person said or did. The action of attacking someone or something. And lastly, an annoyance or resentment brought about by a real or perceived insult to oneself, or one's standards or principles.*

Unfortunately, we have all at one time or another said or done things which were thoughtless, insensitive, or even mean-spirited. When a GirlFriend is committing this *infraction*, sometimes her motive may not be to purposefully Offend you, however, the results are still the same. While we can't control the intentions or behavior of others, we can determine how we will respond when that ball gets *tossed in our lap*. Ok, enough of the sports terminology!

Have any of your GirlFriends ever said or done anything which cut you to the quick, or hurt your feelings? I'm sure they have. It could be as simple as what took place while I was having lunch with a GirlFriend.

After finishing my meal, I decided to splurge and order dessert, which I seldom do. It was my birthday month, and the restaurant was having a special. It was a *sign!* So, What's a Girl to do? Happy Birthday to Me! Even though my GirlFriend refrained from ordering any delicacies, I was more than willing to share mine with her. Maybe I wasn't *more* than willing, but I would have shared a bite, *IF* she *really* wanted it. Ok, so probably *ONLY* if she had asked me!

As I was oohing and umming, after my first fork full, she gave me *that* look. You know the one I mean. Similar to the one your mother gave you after you colored your hair hot pink as a teenager. It's the same glare you would give your dog if you caught him with what was left of your new Jimmy Choo shoes ~ *if* only. You know the squinting of the eyes, and the pursing of the lips, which says you did something really bad, and now you're in big trouble!

Next, she went on to give me this long commentary of the 25 reasons why I *should no*t be eating this fabulous, mouth watering, seven-layer chocolate cake, with chocolate frosting. You know, the calories, the gluten, the white sugar ~ yada, yada! I personally couldn't even think of *ONE* reason not to eat it. But then again, that's just me! What would motivate someone to sanction me and take away my enjoyment, just because it was not her preference? She was not my mother, she was just my GirlFriend! I felt my blood pressure rising as she went on and on, and it wasn't from the cake either!

So, What's a Girl to DO?

I was faced with a decision. I could react in the *'flesh'*, and tell her what I was truly thinking, or I could respond in the Spirit, by choosing to answer God's way. I recalled a statement Joel Osteen made recently which said, *"Every day we have plenty of opportunities to get angry or Offended."* This was one of those days. He went on to say: *"However, what you do when you indulge in negative emotions, is you give someone or something outside yourself the power over your happiness. You can choose not to let little things upset you."* Hmmmm, that's a good one, Joel.

Based on all that, instead of getting *mad* at her, I decided to focus on the true facts I knew about my friend. She is a 'health nut', has done her homework on nutrition, and has heard me complain about my weight, on numerous occasions. I also reminded myself she meant well, and that she cared about me. It's called perspective. So, with one eyebrow raised, and a half a smile, I thanked her for her concern. I could have very easily gotten upset at my GirlFriend's words, but then again, was I going to give to her the "power over my happiness?" Nope.

Everyone, yes even her, has a right to their own opinion, and despite how I might have felt about hers, she chose to give it to me anyway. In the long run, did it really matter? My selfish, Offended-based reaction could have blown the entire not-a-big-deal situation out of proportion. More than likely we would both have gone away *mad*, which would have left a bad *taste* in both of our mouths. But instead, I asked the server for a box, and took the remainder of my decadent cake home to enjoy it ~ guilt free! Obviously, I was then left with a simply glorious flavor in my mouth instead!

Now, I will say, had that type of dialog continued to be an ongoing habit with her, it would have served us both well to have a difficult conversation concerning it. We'll cover that topic more in the next chapter. As long as we need to interact with others, we will always encounter provocative circumstances and irritating situations.

We don't want to be the sort of Christian girls who make a habit of always being upset with each other or having critical and negative spirits. Just waiting to be Offended is not who God has called us to be, GirlFriends. It certainly is not pleasant being around a *drama queen* like that, let alone acting like one ourselves, right?

What causes us then to let these trivial matters dictate our lives? Having hurt feelings or being easily Offended is almost always a result of being too preoccupied with ourselves. We say things like "She hardly talked to me," "I can't believe she did that to me," or "She doesn't like me." It's all about *ME*! As my amazing husband would say: "What or Who is the *common denominator* here?" *ME*!

Some GirlFriends seem to be walking around with a chip on their shoulder and are very quick to interpret even the most innocent of comments as a justification to be *mad*. They become Offended, not necessarily because of what was said or done to them, but because of their own personal issues. Hurt people, hurt people, and IF we don't learn how to properly deal with our past grievances and emotions, we will find ourselves being easily upset all too often.

We must examine our own heart to see if there is something going on inside of us which causes us to become even more irritable than the situation demands. You know how they say there is a $1000 reaction to a $10 situation. The 'punishment doesn't fit the crime' reaction. In other words, *OVERreaction*! Are we blaming others for Offending us, when in reality we wouldn't be as sensitive in an area if we had addressed those problems already?

Our own insecurities are another cause for us being easily bothered. Our significance gets all tied up with how we think others perceive us, rather than on how we see ourselves, and more importantly how God views us. When we can learn to accept our own imperfections, and those of others, we will become less difficult to Offend, and a much happier GirlFriend to be around.

Not too many people are honestly trying to make our lives miserable. Of course, the Fake and Fatal Friends may be. Remember though, our significance does not come from them either. Ask God to help you overcome those heart wounds, emotional scars and insecurities, so they don't continue to drive a wedge between yourself and your GirlFriends.

Here is another little quiz to see if you get Offended easily.

a. *Do your Girlfriends feel they need to walk on eggshells around you?*

b. *Do you tend to overreact, make mountains out of molehills?*

c. *Do you frequently take comments personally, or in the wrong way?*

d. *Would your Girlfriends describe you as high maintenance?*

e. *Do you place your should or shouldn't rules and expectations on your GirlFriends?*

Jesus even warns His disciples in Luke 17:1, "It is impossible but that Offenses will come." Not gee, what IF they come. No, they *will* inevitably come. Expect it, don't look for it, just know it's a normal part of life. The verse continues to say, "But woe to the one from whom they come."

Which brings us to: What if *YOU* are that person who made an 'off the cuff' comment or Offended a GirlFriend?

It's Story time!

One situation which comes to mind was regarding Jane, one of my Best Friends, at the time. Right in the middle of my *quiet time*, it seemed as if my prayers were 'bouncing off the ceiling', coming back at me. Have you ever felt as if your prayers were somehow not making it to the ears of God? Obviously, He is always there listening, but sometimes there is something in our lives that hinders us from having fellowship with Him! I said to Him, *"Are you there, are you mad at me? If not, why don't I feel as if I am connecting with you?"*

Not in an audible voice, but in my spirit, I heard Him say, *"Yes, I am here, and No, I am not mad at you, but Jane is, and YOU need to go make it right with her."* I'm thinking that she can't be possible because she never mentioned anything to me. I was reminded of the passage in Matthew 5:23-24 which says: "If you are bringing your gift (prayers) to the altar, then suddenly remember your friend has something against you, YOU leave your gift at the altar, and YOU go and apologize and be reconciled. Then come back and offer your gift to God"*!* But I wondered what if she isn't even *mad* at me, I will look like a fool, or worse yet, she might begin to think of something she *could* be *mad* at me about.!"

I decided to put all my excuses aside and be obedient to what I believed God was telling me to do! So, I made the phone call to Jane, and asked her my favorite question. *"Are you Mad at Me?"* To my astonishment, she said, *"Yes, I am."* Obviously, God was right. She went on to explain, in the long version, why she was angry with me. When she had finished, I told her I was sorry I Offended her and asked her if she would be willing to forgive me.

She answered "*NOPE.*" So, to keep our conversation from going to an even worse place, with either one or both of us saying something we would regret, I asked if we could talk about it another time. We agreed on doing that. I just wasn't up for playing the '*You Haven't Suffered Long Enough Game*', or the '*You Need to be Punished More Game!*' You know the ones I mean. Have you ever heard of any of these tactics? Ever played them? Offense or Defense? It's like there are some GirlFriends who seem to find pleasure in hurting you back until you cry 'Uncle'!

I chose to practice Ephesians 4:29, "Let no unwholesome words come out of my mouth, but only what is helpful for building others up." Knowing myself, I knew I was incapable of doing that, in the moment. So, I returned to my praying, and had an awesome time reconnecting with the Lord, until the doorbell rang. It was Jane. We briefly talked about the Offense again, we laughed, we cried, and hugged it out. You can fight to be right, or you can keep the peace! "Be at peace with all women, as much *as* is possible with *YOU!*" Romans 12:18

So, What's a Girl to DO?

Here are some suggestions in approaching a GirlFriend, if you are the Offender?

1. *Confirm your suspicions by sharing what you see. "It looks like what I said Offended or hurt you."*

2. *If she admits to being Offended, don't run away, or immediately try to defend yourself. Instead, begin by saying, "I didn't realize what I said/did was Offensive to you." Say this, only if you didn't know it was.*

3. *Ask a question to get her talking. "What was it I said or did?"*

4. *Validate your GirlFriend by reflecting what you heard her say. If she revealed something about her perspective, be sure to show her you got it. "I get it. You're tired of me being late."*

5. *Learn and adapt. Was there something you now understand better that will cause you to reconsider your position?*

6. *Thank your GirlFriend for the conversation, even if you don't agree with what she said. Just a simple "Thank you for helping me see your point of view" works well.*

7. *Don't contradict the Offended person or tell her why she was wrong. For example, "You can't possibly be offended by THAT!"*

8. *Put yourself in her shoes (hope they're cute) by seeing things from her perspective, not yours.*

As you can see from my experience with Jane, someone can be Offended without you even knowing you were being Offensive. Let me just say that you cannot hold a GirlFriend responsible for Offending you IF you have never been honest enough to tell her how you feel concerning a particular matter.

Your GirlFriends cannot read your mind. IF it wasn't a blatant *foul* she committed, you need to be honest with her about a particular habit or situation. Let her know, in a kind and gentle way, what bothers you *PRIOR* to it building up inside of you, then dumping it out all over her! I can promise you that, it will turn out ugly for both of you, I will cover this in much, much, greater detail later!

How do you know IF a GirlFriend is even mad at you, you might ask? I have created my very own top ten list of some warning signs which might give you a clue.

10. She can't look you in the eye when you're speaking with her.

9. She doesn't return your numerous calls, texts, emails or Facebook messages.

8. She stops talking when you enter the room.

7. She answers your questions with a one-word answer.

6. When she sees you coming, she turns and walks the opposite way.

5. She immediately slams the door in your face after seeing you standing there.

4. She refers to you as her 'Former Friend'.

3. She doesn't invite you to her biggest party of the year, which is on YOUR birthday!

2. She wears a T-shirt that says, "Yes, I am mad at __ " with your name on it.

1. She tells you to your face... "I am soooooo mad at you"!!!

I know, some of these are pretty funny, but I'm sorry to say, many are not!

It's easier for most of us to let Offenses slide off our backs when they are merely annoyances. Obviously, there are situations that happen to us which are far more hurtful and deeply Offensive than those I've mentioned in this chapter. I realize many of them don't have the happy endings we desire either.

Trust me when I say I know how you feel, as I have also experienced the heartbreak of being deeply Offended by close GirlFriends too. What I have learned though, is the godly remedy for dealing with the pain, is it much the same whether it's caused by petty rudeness, or a deep wounded spirit. The latter usually just takes more time to heal.

Feelings such as anger or being *mad* are normal, God-given emotions, and are not wrong in themselves. The key is, we need to learn how to express these feelings appropriately. We've all heard of *What Not to Wear*, here is *What Not to DO* when faced with difficult situations which can cause us to become angry! Even though anger is not sin, it can be used in sinful ways as shown in these verses.

Ephesians 4:26-31 states, "Don't sin by letting anger control you. Don't let the sun go down while you are still angry, for anger gives a foothold to the devil. Don't use foul or abusive language. Let everything you say be good and helpful, so that your words will be an encouragement to those who hear them. And do not bring sorrow to God's Holy Spirit by the way you live. Get rid of all bitterness, rage, anger, harsh words, and slander, as well as all types of evil behavior."

First, pray for God's grace not to 'Internalize' your anger or 'Externalize' it towards others.

- ***Internalizing*** *your anger is expressed by Storing it up, Withdrawing, Creating a Hard Shell, Pretending Everything is Fine, Making digs, Giving the Silent Treatment, or Ruminating in your mind how much you have been hurt. You may look fine outwardly, but it will hurt you physically, emotionally and destroy your friendships.*

- ***Externalizing*** *your anger towards others by being Aggressive, Venting, Retaliating, Gossiping, Expecting, Yelling, Screaming,*

Accusing, Throwing things, Slamming Doors, and even Physical Harm! It hurts you, your reputation, and others.

Next, recognize the goal should *always* be to *solve* the problem, not *hurt* your GirlFriend. Anger must be *under* control at all times, and not *out* of control. The solution for dealing with Offenses are found in the verse that follows: Ephesians 4:32. "Instead, be kind to one another, tenderhearted, forgiving one another, just as God through Christ has forgiven you."

Who gets hurt when you internalize? You do. Who gets hurt when you externalize or vent? They do! When you are Offended, you *WILL* obviously have sad and mad feelings, but they don't need to cause you to act bad. Remember, no one can *MAKE* us angry, they will only bring out what is already inside of us.

I'm sure you know the expression, "If someone hurts you, don't get *mad*, get even." Well, that is the *world's* answer for Offenses, and we can see how well that's been working out! Here is an alternative response you might consider practicing after being Offended by a GirlFriend. Don't get *Mad*, Don't get Even, Don't Condemn, Don't Defend, or Pretend, but look to God, and Choose instead to Amend!

What does this mean in practical terms? It means you have the opportunity to respond in a new and different way to the problem of being Offended. You accomplish that by changing your old way of doing things, and replacing it with God's way of thinking and acting. "Don't be conformed to the standards of this world, but let God transform you inwardly by a complete renewing of your mind. Then you will be able to know the will of God, what is good and is pleasing to Him and is perfect." Romans 12:2

Let me give you a hypothetical example of two ways not to respond to an Offense which could happen between GirlFriends. Now, I'm not saying any of my GirlFriends would ever do anything like this. Even *IF* any of them had, I'm not talking about them! Remember, this is just a pretend case. Wink, wink! Here we go.

The OFFENSE: You have a GirlFriend who is chronically late. IF your tendency is to get frustrated, irritated, and downright *mad* at her, you could react negatively in one of 2 ways.

IF you are an *Internalizer*, here is what you might think, say or do:

You say to yourself while you are waiting for her to pick you up: "I hate being late. She has no respect for me. IF she would have just told me earlier, I could have driven myself to the party. IF she didn't put so much on her plate, this wouldn't have happened. I'm sick and tired of this." Your GirlFriend then pulls up in her car, with a big smile on her face, and gives you her trite "Sorry about that" apology, or maybe says nothing at all. You keep your mouth shut and pretend all is well.

When you get to the party, you roll your eyes and look towards *her* to let your other GirlFriends know *SHE* is the reason you were late. You stuff it inside, and never bring it up to her. That wouldn't be the *Christian thing* to do, so you think. However, *EVERY* single time this happens again (and it will), or you even think about the situation, you get *mad* all over again!

Now, *IF* you are an **Externalizer** type, you might think, say or do:

Your GirlFriend pulls up in her car, you get in and slam the door behind you, as fast and as hard as you possibly can! You actually think you might have thrown your back out of whack doing that! Anyway ~ You begin to rapidly tap your foot on the floorboard, staring down at your watch 1000 times, then glaring over to her, as you shake your head from side to side.

The words flow fast and furiously from your lips, 'shaming and blaming' her for the situation you are in of being late to the party. You yell at her concerning how selfish she is, and how she obviously doesn't respect you or your time. After you get to the party, you walk up to her and throw a glass of punch in her face. Read it again, it's a *glass of punch*! Then, you thrust your head back and laugh, as you watch it run down the front of her beautiful, new Gucci dress. OK, I guess I got a little carried away. You get the idea!

Now, guess what happens the next time either of these scenarios take place? For the *Internalizer*, when her GirlFriend is late again, but the issue was never honestly addressed, probably the same exact scene will transpire. Unless you make the decision *PRIOR* to attack the problem, and not the person, nothing will ever change.

You all know the definition of insanity, right? For the one person who has never heard it's: "Doing the same thing over and over, yet expecting *DIFFERENT* results." It's just not going to happen. Although, I do have a feeling if you are on the receiving end of the *Externalizer's* wrath, you will probably either never be late again, or you will not volunteer to pick her up again ~ and I mean *EVER*!

The question then becomes: What will you *do* with these feelings? Just because you don't deal with the Offenses head on, and you bury these thoughts and emotions, does *NOT* mean you have *let go* of them. Just the opposite. *IF* Offenses, real or imagined, are not dealt with in the proper way, aka God's way, they will build up inside of you, as if you are putting each Offense into a *gunny sack*, or a Michael Kors bag, whichever is available*!*

Then, one day when that bag is full of Offenses, and your GirlFriend says or does just one little thing that bothers you, this nasty bag will rip wide open, spilling everything out you have ever held against her for the past 20 years. Believe me when I say, it will get very ugly!

This reminds me of the verse that says, "It's the little foxes that spoil the vine." Songs of Solomon 2:15. It's not always the huge Offenses, but rather the accumulation of small irritations that will cause the explosions. Trying to overcome Offenses is *NOT* accomplished by holding your thoughts and feelings inside. You're not somehow being more *spiritual*, by engaging in this practice either. It certainly doesn't mean you have forgiven your GirlFriend simply because you have remained silent.

"Speaking the truth, in love", expressed in a humble and gentle way, can help your GirlFriend see from your viewpoint a habit which drives you nuts. It will be a huge help for her to understand what it's like for you to be on the receiving end of the times she chooses to be late. *IF* handled in a Christ-like manner, and if she is a true GirlFriend, you can more than likely count on her to work *together* with you to *solve* the problem, not *hinder* the friendship.

If we act *OUTWARD* with our anger, we could hurt other people, physically and emotionally. If we act *INWARD*, with it all bottled up inside of us, studies have shown we are more prone to depression and other diseases. Thus, besides hurting others by our silence, we will also hurt ourselves.

There is a third option too, in handling Offenses. It's found in Proverbs 19:11 and says, "A person's wisdom makes him slow to anger, and it's to 'her' credit to ignore an Offense." You do realize we are not required by God to confront a GirlFriend every time she Offends us. If that were true, I would be a busy girl, and perhaps a very depressed girl too!

Depending on the situation, sometimes the best course of action is to leave it between her and God. Only you can determine if this Offense is of great enough importance to confront, or if it's something you can honestly let go. There are times when the best thing to say when you are Offended by a GirlFriend is to say ~ *NOTHING* at all!

You may also want to be aware if there are any possible stresses going on in her life causing her to act out in ways which may be unusual for her. In such a situation you are not excusing her actions, but rather, trying to understand her difficult times, and show an abundance of grace.

If you are still not sure which direction to go and it's important to you, it would be valuable for you to seek counsel from a trusted GirlFriend before going forward. Proceed here with much caution, being sure it doesn't turn into a gossip session, as we unpacked in our last chapter.

How do *you* typically respond in cases like these, when you are Offended?

Let's recap some godly practices to consider when you are Offended.

PRAY and let God know how you feel. Ask Him to show you specific ways to respond.

OVERLOOK her Offense, IF you can. "Love covers a multitude of sins." Proverbs 10:12.

REFLECT on any seed of truth in what she said. What might have provoked the Offense? Is there something you could have done to prevent it?

RESIST the urge to defend yourself. This step has been the most difficult for me. I can waste a lot of time and energy on explanations and defenses.

CONSIDER who the other person is. Don't take everything said or done too personally. People are not always out to get you, sometimes, it's a statement about their issues.

SPEAK the truth in love. The Godly approach instead of making it all about you, is to practice directing your anger or frustration toward solving the problem, and restoring the relationship, not about proving your case.

DON'T seek revenge; rather give a blessing instead of a curse.

So, What's a Girl to DO?

---

*Which of your GirlFriends do you think may be mad at you?

---

*What steps can you take to make amends?

_____

Who do you think you may have Offended?

_____

_____

What can you do to make it right with her?

_____

_____

When choosing to participate in this *Offensive Game* in a defensive manner, we are required to play it by *The Book. When* we do, we will *ALL* become the *Real Game Changers* in life!

Elephants Never

Leave a Room

Simply Because We

Act as Though

They're Not There!

CHAPTER 5
Where's the Elephant?

"Speaking the truth in love, we may grow up in all things into Him."

Ephesians 4:15

There are those obvious situations which happen between GirlFriends, we would just rather not talk about! I mean it, literally. You know, those dreaded delicate conversations, misunderstandings, assumptions, presumptions and perceptions! *UGH*! We hope, and even pray, they will go away on their own, but unfortunately, they seldom do. What we're talking about here is the *Elephant* in the middle of the room.

Just imagine there is an extremely large, yet darling *Elephant* dressed in the sweetest, pink lace tutu you ever did see! These are the times I wish I could simply insert an emoji here. However, don't let this fashionista fool you. Despite her cute and silent demeanor, if she's not dealt with in a *mammoth* way, she can leave a path of destruction between you and your GirlFriends so wide the bridge may never be gapped. So, some of you may be wondering who or what is this *Elephant* we are talking about. Please, let me explain!

DEFINITION of the ELEPHANT in the ROOM:

Wikipedia describes it this way: *The term refers to a question, problem, solution, or controversial issue which is obvious to everyone who knows about the situation. It is deliberately ignored because to* do otherwise would cause great embarrassment, sadness, arguments, or it is simply too taboo to even bring up.

The Cambridge Dictionary defines it as: An obvious problem or difficult situation that people know about, but do not want to talk about.

We all know elephants can grow up to 14 feet tall and weigh approximately 15,000 lbs. I've always wondered how they get so huge just eating vegetables. It's one of the reasons I try to Avoid them at all costs. No, not the *Elephants* silly, the vegetables! So, as you can see, any *Elephant* would typically be seen and acknowledged, except in this case, of course. Since *it* stands right smack in the middle of a room, in order to avoid it, we will need to do whatever it takes to walk around it, step over it, crawl under it or simply close our eyes to the fact that it's even there.

Most of the time the subject we are trying to steer clear of is *heavy*, and no one wants to move it, disturb it or even touch it with a ten-foot pole. This is a huge misconception, though, because we tend to think we're taking the easy way out by denying or running away from it. But, in reality, what we're really doing is allowing the situation to build up, making it even more difficult to approach the problem later. Even though misunderstandings may begin as small baby *Elephants,* they can grow larger over time, especially when they're *fed* with Avoidance or assumptions. By the way, in the event you haven't noticed, these *Elephants* never leave the room just because you pretend they aren't there! We touched on this topic in the last chapter.

Please let me explain the dynamics of this Avoidance *Game*. It could start with a *funny face* look, an attitude, or a disconnection when you're with a GirlFriend. Maybe it's a feeling you can't put your finger on, or even worse, an out and out disagreement you had. The longer you ignore it, the more it *weighs* down your relationship. In fact, once this *giant* finds a welcoming home, she tends to stick around for a very long time, and sometimes will even take up permanent residence, *if* you let her.

Let's say for example, you're out for an evening with a GirlFriend who has a terminal illness. If you *NEVER* bring up the fact that she is dying, then *that* topic becomes the *Elephant* in the room. Avoiding it will cause you to tiptoe around the conversation, talking about any and everything except the most important thing going on in her life right then.

Instead of having a free-flowing conversation, your time together is mostly spent *dancing* around the issue. You convince yourself to carefully *weigh* your every word, not wanting to step on your GirlFriend's toes or make her feel uncomfortable. However, isn't this Avoidance the very thing that causes our interactions with one another to be somewhat shallow and superficial?

It's more likely than not that you are both thinking about the *Elephant* anyway. Obviously, timing here is critically important, and sometimes it's best to let some *Elephants* lie quietly on the sofa until they can be safely approached. On the flip side, couldn't this perhaps be the perfect moment to acknowledge her illness, and openly share your hearts with one another, while there is still opportunity?

These are not easy situations, and hopefully most of the difficult conversations you encounter with others will not be this dire. Perhaps, it's speaking with a GirlFriend about her excessive drinking or her negative attitude. Maybe, you have concerns about a relationship she is getting involved in, or are upset about a comment she made to you. IF these types of situations are handled correctly and with pure motives, our being honest can actually deepen the bonds we have. Isn't that what we all want anyway? Do you care enough to endure these challenging exchanges?

I am not encouraging you to have this type of dialogue with Fringe Friends or non personal relationships, even though the same principles may apply. We are focusing on the walls we allow to build up between real GirlFriends or people we love, which for one reason or another, never get dealt with. The mere fact you find a conversation difficult to approach, can be a sign the issue is important enough to consider talking about.

Good communication is the key to successful relationships. Avoidance ruins honesty, and there can be no real communication without the truth. This isn't about being *brutally* honest, but rather *truly* honest. Iyanla Vanzant says when we have important relationships that need our attention, instead of calling them confrontations, which can sound mean or intimidating, she calls them '*CAREfrontations.*' I love that! Thanks, Iyanla.

Some of us have been taught, either by words or example, to *Repress* our feelings rather than to *Express* them concerning sensitive matters. Because of our *Don't Rock the Boat* mentality, or of being overly concerned about how our Girlfriends might view us, we may choose to *Protect* rather than *Connect*, playing the *Keep it to Ourselves Game*. As we learned in prior chapters, either of these ways of dealing with our emotions will have negative results.

John Powell wrote in his book *Why Am I Afraid to Tell You Who I Am* "Most of us feel that others will not be able to tolerate emotional honesty. We would rather defend our dishonesty on the grounds that it might hurt others, and having rationalized our phoniness into nobility, we settle for superficial relationships." I couldn't have said that better myself, John!

So, if it is so important to keep the peace, and speak the truth in love, as our *Focus Verse* suggests, why don't we? Let me share with you 4 possible reasons why we resist engaging the *Elephants*. Circle the areas which keep you from having the *'Carefrontations'* you've been resisting.

SCARED:

The number one reason is *FEAR*! That's understandable, it can be pretty scary. We *DO* need to proceed with caution and count the costs before getting into conversations which are unpredictable. I definitely struggle with this insecurity when it comes to engaging in those difficult talks. Usually my first tendency in dealing with an *Elephant* is to run away and hide. It's pretty much my second, third, and fourth choice too!

We Avoid these uncomfortable conversations for fear of how our GirlFriends might react. If we *rattle her cage*, we risk having her see us in a negative light or worse yet, she gets *mad* at us. It *IS* possible there could be fallout from being honest, making matters worse. This can still happen despite being well intentioned and saying all the right things in the best possible way. *'Carefrontations'* don't always lead to the resolutions we want or expect.

It's the reason we need to enter that *room* with vigilance. *Things* can happen when we try to move an *Elephant* out of her comfort zone or disturb her in any way, and we sure don't want to get trampled on in the process. I can't state enough times that we all have a desire to be valued and accepted, not only from our GirlFriends, but by anyone we hold near and dear to our hearts. Case in point:

My husband grew up in a home with a father who was physically and verbally abusive. That was not my experience, thank God, but it didn't take me long to figure out how to 'jump through the right hoops'. Understanding that, we did everything we could to avoid upsetting him, being careful to tread lightly with particular topics in his presence. As long as we *towed the line*, and played by the Avoidance rules, all went well. Do you have any GirlFriends you need to do this *twisted dance* for? I can assure you, this is *NOT* a fun ritual.

While visiting with his parents several years ago, we got into a very personal conversation, right before retiring for the evening. The statement was made by his father, that because I was not *blood* or his *real* family, I would be left out of his will. I could have cared less about the will, but I was devastated to hear he did not consider me his *real* family. After all, it wasn't as if we were strangers. I had been married to their son for a very long time!

I didn't respond immediately, probably because I think I was still in shock by his insensitive words. Secondly, I was smart enough to be afraid. Very afraid! I had already been disowned by him several times before for giving my unasked-for opinion. But this comment, made in my presence, was so painful to me, yet he thought nothing of it. You see, he had been the only man I considered and called *Dad* for nearly 30 years.

I was hurt, sad and really *MAD*! Prior to going to sleep that evening, I informed my husband I was going to talk with his father about my feelings in the morning. He insisted I do *NO* such thing! Now remember, *Elephants* stand about 14 feet tall, weigh approximately 15,000 pounds, and when untamed, they can leave a path of devastation like no other.

However, *IF* left unattended, they will go wherever they please and wreak havoc on everyone and everything that gets in their way. My husband knew this *Elephant's* rampage all too well and didn't want to cause such a stampede on *US*!

I tossed and turned and didn't sleep much, thinking of how he didn't consider me his daughter. *Could* I have dismissed it as that's just who he is? *Should* I just let it go? I decided I could *NOT*. Just before breakfast the next morning, I again firmly stated to my husband I had prayed about it, and even though I was shaking in my sandals, and even though he was against it, I was going forward with my plan.

If you know me at all, then you know I'm a big scaredy-cat, and it would be highly unusual that I would rush into a '*lion's den*' or go against what my husband's desires. I was fully aware of the possible consequences, but for some reason, I *knew* it was exactly what God wanted me to do.

As we were leaving our room the next morning, I repeated several times in my head: "God has not given me a spirit of fear, but of power, love, and a sound mind." 2 Timothy 1:7. Did I mention my father-in-law had been the recipient of several Golden Glove awards.....in *BOXING*! Even into his 80s, his muscles were as hard as rocks and at that moment, they were beginning to look more like boulders to me!

As I began gently sharing with him how I was feeling, I was immediately met with much opposition from him, and even my mother-in-law came to his defense. It was all quite a blur, but I continued sharing nevertheless in a quiet, concise and controlled manner. When I was finished, he never said he was sorry or that he understood how I could feel that way. But the good news is, I was still alive! So, for me, I considered that a *WIN*.

My father-in-law was never a huggy-kissy or a wear his heart on his sleeve kind of guy, so I never expected any of those responses from him. In all the years I knew him, he never told me he loved me, and that was ok too. I was aware he had a difficult life growing up, and I was sure he had never heard any words of love or affirmation spoken to him.

When we were leaving to return home that day, he gave me a look I hadn't seen before, so I was beginning to get a little nervous. Then, it happened. No, he didn't have his boxing gloves on. Instead, he came towards me and gave me a hug, and whispered softly, "*I Love You!*" Beginning that day, our relationship became more genuine and heartfelt. I love you too and miss you, *Dad*.

I'm so thankful I took the risk. A big risk, with a huge reward! Even when everyone and everything inside of you is screaming ; 'No, no, don't do it, don't say it,' *IF* you believe God is directing you to confront an *Elephant*, go for it! It's amazing what HE can do when we are obedient to Him, even when the outcome is unpredictable.

It's okay to do it afraid, because He is with you, and has already gone before you to prepare the way. "Trust in the Lord with all your heart, and lean not on your own understanding. In all your ways acknowledge Him, and He will direct your paths." Proverbs 3:5.

UNPREPARED:

I would say another big reason we want to leave the *Elephant* alone, and Avoid certain conversations, is we don't know what to say or how to say it. We simply are not skilled and don't know where to begin. It's not like we were ever taught in school how to relate in a positive manner with others, especially during conflict. Although I think it would have been more beneficial to us than studying Calculus! When was the last time you used that?

Regrettably, we have all been in situations before, when things didn't go as we had planned, and we certainly don't want to repeat that scene. Maybe you didn't say what you really meant to say or you said something you should not have said. GirlFriends, even when there is an *Elephant* that needs our attention, I think most of us genuinely don't want to hurt each other.

If you grew up in a household where 'handling' a situation meant yelling and getting into people's faces or giving them a 'piece of your mind', I can understand why you would feel unprepared to go forward in dealing with the *Elephants*. Perhaps you never learned the difference between *attacking* the person, or *addressing* the problem, being *assertive* instead of being *aggressive*.

Because of these reasons, it's tempting to allow some conversations to be ignored. We choose to Avoid the discomfort that facing it could cause us. It's somewhat like when we have a toothache. We keep taking aspirin to kill the pain, but we never take care of the *root of* the problem by going to the dentist. *UGH!* Believe me when I tell you, the pain will not go away on its own. More than likely they will both get worse over time, if ignored. It's best to deal with the tooth and the *Elephant* as soon as possible.

I've heard Joyce Meyer say there are two kinds of pain: "The pain of moving forward, and the pain of remaining where you are at. Whichever is stronger will probably be the choice you will make, on most occasions." Pain is inevitable, but misery is not. Whether it's handling a difficult encounter or learning the correct way to express our feelings, it's a process which takes time and practice.

UNAWARE:

When communication stops, all sorts of assumptions and presumptions can be inserted into a relationship. The thesaurus explains assumptions as "Something that is accepted as true, but without proof." The fact is, we all make assumptions about people, conversations, and circumstances, whether we realize it or not. We all assume and we judge without knowing all the facts. Let me share yet another personal story, which has a powerful ending, regarding assumptions, presumptions, and projections.

I used to own a lovely Victorian Tea Room with two of my GirlFriends. My friend, Terri, called one afternoon and ordered 50 egg salad sandwiches for a party at her workplace. Obviously, we ordered and received all the yummy ingredients to prepare those for her. However, two days prior to pick up day, she called and canceled the entire order. I guess the men decided they preferred pizza. I'm with them on that one! I said, "*No problem*" and never gave it a second thought.

Over the years, whenever I bumped into Terri, I would always invite her to any upcoming women's events and to my weekly Book Club. Even though her sister Susan attended regularly, Terri never accepted any of my invitations. I assumed she was extremely busy. However, one evening to my delight, she showed up.

We were discussing Matthew 18:15: "If you know your 'sister' has something against you, YOU go and be reconciled." Our in-class assignment was to make a list of those girls we knew or believed might be *mad* at us. We were to contact one girl on the list during the week to make amends with her. We all prayed together, and I said I looked forward to hearing how God would bring freedom and healing to whoever dared to trust Him.

Done, right? Of course not!

Immediately following class, Terri asked if I had a few minutes to talk in private. Obviously, I said "Yes". After everyone had left, I asked her what was going on. She told me how the topic at hand had deeply impacted her. She shared how she felt compelled to speak to the person on the top of her list. I told her I was proud of her. She then looked down, as if looking at her notes, looked back up at me and announced: "*YOU, are the person at the top of my list!*" How on earth do I get myself into these predicaments?

There was a huge *Elephant* in the middle of *my* living room, and I was *IT*! I asked her why I deserved that not so coveted top spot. She asked me if I remembered the tearoom situation 5 years prior. I said I vaguely did. She said she wanted to apologize for cancelling her order and asked if I would forgive her! I laughed. (Please, don't do that when someone is sharing their heart with you.) SHE wanted to apologize to ME! Whew, what a relief.

I asked her why she felt a need to bring it up, after all these years. She went on to explain how she *knew* how mad I *MUST* have been at her. She knew, beyond a shadow of doubt! She also informed me of all the times she Avoided being around me and refrained from going places she knew I would be, which in those days, was just about everywhere.

Still somewhat confused by her reaction to the situation, I asked if it was my response to her, at that time, which led her to believe I was upset with her. She said, "*No, you were very nice. You just laughed and said you would be having a special on egg salad sandwiches for the next couple days!*" I confirmed I had never thought about it again since our phone conversation that day. I reassured her that I forgave her, and from that moment on she was released from ever thinking about it again.

The look on her face was priceless. I could physically see the *heavy* burden she had been carrying for years being lifted. The *weight* of her made up story, in her own mind, was gone and she was now free. John 8:32 says, "You will know the Truth, and the Truth will set you free."

Still trying to understand how this misunderstanding could have happened, I pressed her further by asking her: "*IF this situation had been reversed, and I was the one who cancelled 50 sandwiches from your tearoom, how would you have responded?*" She said ~ wait for it ~ "I *would have been MADDER than a wet hornet!*" Bingo.

Assumptions, Presumptions, and Projections. Proverbs 13:10 says, "With presumption comes nothing but strife, but with wise counsel comes wisdom." Can you see the needless strife and pain it caused her? What had happened? For years she pointlessly suffered and missed out on so many wonderful experiences and friendships because she believed a lie! Armed with our own thoughts and ideas, we connect the dots that aren't really there. We jump to *conclusions* that are really *illusions*, which ultimately leads to *confusion*.

Why and how do assumptions start?

It's easy to make assumptions. All you need is incomplete information about a situation, and an unwillingness, or lack of courage to ask the right questions you need to find the truth. As with any possible reaction to disturbing the *Elephant* in a room, she was afraid to speak with me because she didn't want to deal with the assumed results. Knowing how *SHE* would have responded, and believing I would do the same, assumptions and projections allowed her to hide behind her own version of a story.

Thank you Terri for coming to my home that evening, and for being courageous enough to have that meaningful '*Carefrontation*' with me. We BOTH learned a lot from that one!

So, What's a Girl to DO?

What can we all do to keep similar unnecessary breaks in friendships and misunderstandings from happening? That's correct. Go to the source. Not to your other GirlFriends or to carry the story inside yourself for perhaps *years*!

Can you remember a time, when you assumed something to be true, but it turned out to be completely false? What happened?

DON'T CARE:

I know this may seem like a strange reason we don't deal with issues we know are there. It's probably not as uncommon as you might believe. Don't care? No, it's not that we don't care about our GirlFriends, but rather we don't care to deal with some situations at hand. We don't need to have challenging conversations with everyone you don't see eye to eye with. Being direct is usually your best option, but it's not the *ONLY* one or always the right one either.

Sometimes after *weighing* a circumstance thoroughly, and its possible outcome, most people's preferred way of handling the *Elephant is* choosing the path of least resistance. Avoiding controversies is simply the easiest road to walk. Just forget about it! It's just not worth it! If you feel that way, you are not alone.

Occasions arise when the depth of the relationship may not be significant enough to confront a situation. It will cost us time, thought, energy, and emotional stamina when getting involved in these delicate issues. However, even if we choose not to take action, simply thinking about these sorts of situations over and over, can still take up enormous amounts of brain space. I don't know about you, but I don't have too much extra time or brain space to dedicate to every matter that could come up between GirlFriends. What about you?

Perhaps your GirlFriend *doesn't care* to hear about the problem. Those are the times we need to allow her choices to impact her life, without us being involved. Pray for her and give her the space she may need to process the issues herself. Proverbs 23:9 says: "You cannot speak into the ears of a fool."

We all put expectations on people. The problem is we usually don't communicate those unspoken expectations to each other. Yet, when our GirlFriend doesn't do something we want or *expect* her to, we get disappointed and *mad* at her. She may have absolutely no idea there is an *Elephant in the room*, or what the *Elephant is* because what's important to you, is not a high priority on her list.

We might even say to ourselves, she *should* have known, or it's only common sense. Maybe for *you* it is, however, we are all different. IF a GirlFriend continues to step on our expectations, it might be because we have not done a good enough job sharing those with her. The time to talk about it is not immediately after an event took place. We need to choose a time when we are not still emotionally disturbed by it. If our timing is not right, talk about a stampede!

Based on our perception and assumptions, we will often put an *unachievable* expectation on a GirlFriend. However, when those expectations are not based in reality and agreement, they can become relationship killers. To bring clarity to a situation, I recommend 'communication', not 'confrontation'! There's a *huge* distinction between the two.

Like any new skill, there are strategies for dealing with our GirlFriends more effectively. Learning how to handle conflict or should I say *'careflict'* is not only listening to the words a GirlFriend says, but also hearing her heart.

So, What's a Girl to DO?

How can we eliminate these *Elephants*? Creighton Abrams says, "When eating an elephant, take one bite at a time." Here's a *Game* plan I put together to effectively deal with the *Elephants*.

Acknowledge the Elephant: *Verify if there's a real Elephant there. Letting go of denial is just the first step to healing. Determine if there's a need to address the issue.*

Pray for Wisdom: *Prayer is always your first line of defense and offense. What is God's best method for dealing with it? Speaking up or choosing grace by overlooking it. Do NOT proceed until you are sure God has gone before you. Pray for the best outcome; however, be prepared for the worst.*

Count the Cost: *Is it worth it? Consider the possible outcome and any complications. Are you willing to live with the possible results?*

Determine your Motives: *Never get into a 'carefrontation' to get something off your chest or give someone a piece of your mind. The purpose is always to benefit the other person and the friendship! What are your intentions? What do you hope to accomplish? This is not a dumping ground. If you are going to assume anything at all about your GirlFriend, always assume the best.*

Plan ahead: *Ask for a meeting in person and in private. Pick a convenient time and place, free of distractions. Turn off your phone! Be sure to allow enough time. Say something, like: "I would LOVE to get together over coffee sometime," rather than, "We need to TALK!"*

Control your Emotions: *Make it safe to talk openly about the elephant by remaining calm. Be sure the pitch of your voice doesn't rise. EEEK! IF you are still angry, this is not the time for a beneficial conversation. Share your feelings of how it affected you, in a loving and gentle manner. Use "I feel" rather than "You said or you did." No playing the Shame and Blame game. You can't control how someone else reacts, however, you have an important role by sharing your concern in a loving and non-threatening manner. Colossians 4:6:* "Let your speech always be with grace, as though seasoned with salt, so that you will know how you should respond to each person."

Be Clear and Concise: *Acknowledge the awkwardness the situation created. Get to the heart of the matter. Know exactly what you are going to say; this is not the time to play it by ear or speak everything that's on your mind. Write it down, and rehearse it, if you must. What are the facts? Avoid assumptions. Confine the meeting to ONE issue at a time only. Stay away from all the times it happened in the past. Be direct, honest and detailed, yet kind.*

Attack the problem, and not your GirlFriend. This is a time to make your relationship better, not worse. Be truly honest, but not brutally honest. Don't use "You always or you never."

Listen: *Be empathetic. Hear her side. Don't be defensive. We all have blind spots. Be sure to let her share how she saw the situation. Avoid negative facial expressions, like rolling your eyes. Accept that her perspective may be different than yours. Just because it's not the same, does not mean she is wrong. It's not really about who's right or wrong, anyway. Resist the urge to interrupt. I confess I am the biggest offender with this one. When I was a new Christian, I got very excited because I thought I possessed one of the spiritual gifts listed in the bible. Then, someone pointed out to me that I misread it. It's the gift of Interpretation, NOT the gift of Interruption! Hey, it looked pretty close to me!*

Have an Action Plan: *Don't get stuck going over and over the specifics of the same problem. Find a remedy to the problem soon by saying: "What can WE do differently moving forward?" Plan out clear, next steps of action. Unresolved disagreements leave everyone feeling worse than before. The entire purpose of a 'Carefrontation' is coming to a resolution. Agree together on how you can BOTH keep this from happening again. What did you both learn from it?*

Leave on a Positive Note: *Pray together. It's almost impossible to be mad at someone when praying with and for one another. Each girl must be willing to apologize and forgive one another for their part. It takes two to maintain a healthy friendship. It's important that you both give a little. Thank each other for caring enough to call out the Elephant.*

So, What's a Girl to DO?

Can you think of a difficult conversation you have been putting off having with a GirlFriend? Who is it and what do you need to discuss with her? What's preventing you from doing this?

_____

_____

No matter how you choose to deal with the *Elephants* in your life, Ephesians 4:2 encourages us to, "Always be humble and gentle. Be patient with each other, making allowance for each other's faults because of your love."

Restoring and retaining your relationship with a GirlFriend should be first and foremost of importance when addressing an *Elephant*. False assumptions and presumptions can ruin a reputation and a friendship. Perhaps now is the time to open the door wide and gently, yet firmly, escort that *Elephant* out of the room, and say Bye-Bye Felicia!

Jealousy Happens When

We Focus on

Our GirlFriend's Blessings,

Rather than

our Own!

CHAPTER 6
Eat Your Heart Out!

"Where there is Jealousy and selfish ambition, there is disorder and every evil thing."

James 3:16

L et's talk about Jealousy. Yep, that green-eyed monster is lurking around every corner, just waiting to reveal its ugly head. Everyone experiences Jealousy or Envy to some degree, even though we may not want to admit it! In a way, it's almost worse than being *mad* or upset with your GirlFriend, because it's *YOU* who caused this one, all by your lonesome self. It's not as if she's talking bad about you or *making* you feel this way.

I know what you might be thinking. Isn't it your GirlFriend who is provoking you to become Jealous? I'm sorry to inform you, but *most* of the time, not really. Of course, there will always be those girls who make things more difficult on us, by being boastful, competitive or seemingly oblivious to our feelings. In that case, you may want to consider if they are your real GirlFriends or Fake Friends.

While we are often tempted to place the blame on someone else, these awful feelings typically stem from something deep inside of *us*. They are essentially the result of our own discontentment with ourselves or our circumstances. Instead of feeling or reacting in a negative way when confronted with Envy or Jealousy, we can use it as a motivation to make positive changes in our own lives. When we see certain attributes a GirlFriend exhibits, instead of comparing our lives to hers, we can challenge ourselves to work harder in those areas we want to improve on.

Now, I don't believe anyone wakes up in the morning saying, "Well, today is the day I'm going to feel Envious of my Girlfriend or her happiness!" At least, I hope not! But, why is it then we still struggle with these feelings even when a GirlFriend has been nothing but kind, loving, and supportive of us?

We'll discover that and more in the following pages as we uncover: The Differences between Envy and Jealousy, Why GirlFriends get Jealous, Identify ways we act out, and Determine what a Girl can DO when dealing with this *Competition Game.* Let's begin with the official definitions of Envy and Jealousy

DEFINITION of JEALOUSY:

Wikipedia explains it as: *Referring to the thoughts or feelings of insecurity, fear, and concern over a lack of possessions. Jealousy can consist of one or more emotions such as anger, resentment, inadequacy, or helplessness. Jealousy, nicknamed the green-eyed monster by Shakespeare, involves wanting to hold on to what you do have, either a possession, person, or position. Jealousy in the broader sense could also be fear of losing attention, being possessive or protective.*

DEFINITION of ENVY: *An emotion which occurs when a person lacks another person's superior qualities, achievements, or possessions and either desires it for themselves, or wishes the other didn't have it".*

It seems pretty straightforward, so why all the confusion? In its original meaning, Jealousy is very distinct from Envy, but the two terms have popularly become synonymous in the

English language. So, we'll *try* to use them in that way in this chapter. Simply put:

*** *Jealousy* is a reaction to the threat of losing something (or someone) you have.

*** *Envy* is a reaction to wanting something someone else has. It's similar to coveting.

You could say Jealousy and Envy are kind of like first cousins. Either way you look at it, neither are honorable characteristics to possess, nor is it healthy to be Jealous of our GirlFriends! Both emotions, if left unchecked, have the potential to cause great harm to you, and to all who play this *Game* with you.

Not only will they cause intense anxiety, obsessive thoughts, and difficulty concentrating, they can affect you physically, as well. Things like increased heart rate, sweating, and feeling sick to your stomach are all common bodily responses to Envy and Jealousy. Scientists have also proven these two characters can cause headaches, weight loss or gain, and even chest pains. Proverbs 14:30 states "A heart at peace gives life to the body, but Envy rots the bones." Thus the title of this chapter, *Eat Your Heart Out!*

These cousins are nothing new, though. They've been around since shortly after the first woman was created. In fact, the competition between the first two siblings ever born turned deadly, because of Envy. Talk about "disorder and every evil thing," as stated in our *Focus Verse*. It doesn't get much worse than killing your own brother! Genesis 4 tells the story of how Cain killed Abel, because he was Envious that God accepted his brother's offering, but not his. That's taking this *Competitive Game* to a whole nother level. Unfortunately, in this situation, they both lost that contest.

Do you know what God said to Cain immediately after He rejected his offering? He said, "Why are you so dejected and discouraged? Don't you know if you will *DO* right, then you will *feel* right." So, instead of Cain looking inward, changing his attitude, and improving his own behavior for the next opportunity, he made the *fatal* decision to *eliminate* the problem that made him feel *less than.* Namely, his brother!

Well, a little more updated story of Jealousy was relayed to me when I recently asked my then 10-year-old granddaughter, Annie, if she ever felt Jealous. She immediately said, *"Yes, I used to feel Jealous sometimes when a GirlFriend got what I wanted, when she looked nicer than me, or when she was better at doing something, like dancing."* Now, that's a young girl who is honest, and in touch with her feelings. We could all take a lesson from her on that!

She went on to tell the story of one Christmas Eve, when she was *much* younger, and our family was opening gifts together. We do this one person at a time, so we can appreciate each gift, and the giver too. Her cousin, my other 10-year-old granddaughter Chloe, who is equally as smart and beautiful, had just received a *SnackEez* as a gift. In the event you are as uninformed as I was, she described it as a combination cup and attached straw, with a separate section for a snack. One stop snacking! Hey, I'm Jealous, I want one of those too!

Now, because Annie wanted one too but didn't receive it, she began to fuss and cry. Shortly after her Mom settled her down, and it was her turn to unwrap her next gift, she was elated to find ~ you guessed it ~ a *SnackEez*! Whew, no pressure here. It starts early, GirlFriends!

This opportunity was too good to pass up, so I asked her the next question. *"Now that you're 'older' what do you do when you start to feel Jealous?"* Annie answered very quickly: *"I pray, and ask God to help me not to be Jealous. I try to get over it and be happy for her."*

Her big brother, Alex (my also intelligent and handsome, 13-year-old grandson) chimed in with: *"I actually like to say to my friends out loud, 'What a great job you did or I am happy for you'."* He continued to say, *"At first you may still feel a little Jealous, but soon after, you REALLY will be happy for them."*

You might be thinking: "Isn't that being a bit hypocritical?" I can understand how you might think that. However, doing what God says to do in His Word is never being hypocritical. It's being obedient, and that's always the right thing to *DO*. The bible makes it very clear when it admonishes us to "Rejoice with those who rejoice." Romans 12:15. There is no addendum at the end of that verse saying: but *only* IF you feel like it. No, it's whether we feel like it, or not!

The last lesson my grandkids taught me that day was their final statement on the subject. Almost simultaneously they said: *"And remember to always be grateful for what you DO have!"* I must say, their grandparents, I mean their parents, sure did a wonderful job raising those little *wise* guys! Ha! Honestly, with their amazing insights, I could end this chapter now, and you would have enough information to deal effectively with Envy and Jealousy. However, I won't. Sometimes situations are a bit more complicated with our GirlFriends, therefore, I will continue. Besides, I need a whole lot more pages to fill this chapter!

So, what about you, and me? Do we ever get involved with this *I Want What She Has Game* with our GirlFriends? In order to deal with these emotions effectively, it's important we identify the root cause of our Jealousy or Envy. Let's highlight a couple of the main underlying reasons we feel this way towards our GirlFriends, who we do actually care about.

FEAR:

One of the main causes of Jealousy is *FEAR*. As you saw from our last chapter, fear is at the core of many issues we need to work through. In the case of Jealousy, it may stem from losing someone or something important to you in your past, and now you're afraid of it happening again. Wherever the fear comes from, it can make us more guarded, mistrustful, and cause us to feel insecure, especially in our relationships. We wonder things like: 'What if a Girlfriend decides to spend more time with another friend other than me?'

It seems to me, we only have two choices when that happens. First is, we can *choose* to be Jealous or Envious. However, the negative results of those emotions will cause us either to withdraw or be more possessive of our friends. Fear will cause us to hold on tighter to our friendship, thinking it will make it stronger. However, the exact opposite will happen. Your GirlFriends will begin to feel smothered and controlled, and I can guarantee you, Jealousy will destroy your relationship, if you don't reign in that type of behavior.

The second alternative, and the better response is to learn how to deal with the fact that our fears could genuinely be realized. If that's what takes place, then our part to play would be acceptance. It doesn't necessarily mean she likes someone else more than you or that you will necessarily lose your friendship with her. The reality could be they have other things in common or there is a different dimension to their relationship other than what the two of you enjoy together.

You can't expect or put pressure on any one GirlFriend to be your 'be all, end all' person. You need to release her and give her the freedom to choose who she wants to spend her time with. People are not possessions, and we all need that same flexibility in our relationships. It's healthy to have a variety of GirlFriends, and a wide circle of friends, who make our lives more interesting and balanced.

Everyone assigns their own value to a friendship, and it's very subjective and personal. Have you ever been in a situation where you called one of your GirlFriends your Best Friend, however, you were *NOT* her best friend? Not only could that be awkward, it can be potentially hurtful, *IF* you allow it to be. The difference lies in how you decide to deal with that truth.

I don't believe there is anything you can do to change the situation, but you can and must be sure to change your self-talk. You need to learn how to gracefully and confidently accept the relationship for what it is. Work on being the very best person and friend you can be, and enjoy each of your GirlFriends for who they are, with no strings attached.

Just a little side note here. I know it might sound a bit hypersensitive, but please allow me to give you a little suggestion. When you introduce your BFF to your circle of friends, you might want to be aware of the feelings of your other more sensitive GirlFriends. Perhaps you might want to say she is *one* of my Best Friends or *one* of my Favorite people. It allows others to feel they are not left out or *less than*. Just sayin'. "Look out not only for your own interests, but also the interests of others." Philippians 2:4

Fearing the loss of stature can also cause us to become Jealous. I have seen and heard of scenarios such as this taking place in friendships, in the business world, and even with those in high profile positions. If you're a leader, sometimes you may feel threatened when the *new girl* comes into your group, and others gravitate towards her, instead of you. This can also be of concern if you are the *unspoken* point person in your *'tribe'* of GirlFriends. I think you all know who you are, right?

I have a friend who recently joined a new church. She, along with the rest of her family, were well known and respected in their local Christian community. After receiving the pastor's blessing, she became involved in teaching ladies' groups. She eventually gained a large circle of friends who came to her class regularly. Just as they had done in prior churches they attended, my friend and her husband opened their home for bible studies, along with doing social activities together.

One day the pastor's wife invited my GirlFriend over for coffee (it's not me). She assumed it was for a friendly visit to get to know her better. She was disappointed when the pastor's wife informed her that she did not feel *comfortable* concerning the connections she was making at church, and wanted her to stop. Of course, my friend told her she was sorry she felt that way, as she had no ulterior motive. She purely wanted to 'come alongside' the leadership, and encourage women to have a closer walk with the Lord.

The pastor's wife confessed she had *felt* her position was being jeopardized, and even went so far as to say she was Jealous of my friend's popularity and influence. For obvious reasons, my friend left that church. How sad. Instead of cheering her on, and seeing my GirlFriend as a blessing and a co-laborer in Christ, she allowed her own fears, insecurities, and Jealousy to control her emotions. Relationships can be eaten away by the destructive power of unchecked Envy or Jealousy.

So, What's a Girl to DO?

The antidotes for overcoming fear in relationships are:

1. Letting go of past hurts and experiences.

2. Understanding God's acceptance of You.

3. Having confidence in who you are, and your relationships.

4. Giving up control of others.

5. Enlarging your circle of friends.

Low self image:

American essayist, Joan Didion, puts it this way when describing another cause of Jealousy: *"Pure Jealousy is to see it for what it is. A dissatisfaction with oneself."* In the *olden days,* we used to call this an inferiority complex. That's actually a pretty good description. Having an inferior view of yourself is characterized by a lack of confidence and feeling badly about who you are.

You believe you will never be good enough, or measure up to someone else's standards, or even the ones you set for yourself. Do you frequently compare yourself to others, believe most people don't like you, focus heavily on your weaknesses, or change your opinions or personality in order to be accepted? If you answered yes to these questions, you may struggle with a low self-esteem.

Sometimes these feelings are formed in our childhood. It's helpful to figure out where your Jealousy or Envy might stem from, such as a history of failures or personal rejections. Maybe you had poor grades in school, had weight issues, or lived with 'critical parents'. Perhaps, it began when the all star football player you were madly in love with in high school, took your GirlFriend to the homecoming dance, while you sat home *eating your heart out* with a party size bag of potato chips, and a half gallon of heavenly hash ice cream. OK, enough about me!

All kidding aside, there are situations, which happen in our lives, which can directly affect the way we view ourselves. They cause us to doubt ourselves and bring us to the conclusion that we don't have what it takes to succeed in life. Self-esteem is determined by seeing ourselves the way we are now, and comparing it to how we would be if we were perfect! In the event you haven't noticed, there is no one who is perfect! Even though we can't change the circumstances which cause us to believe we have no value, we can learn to stop focusing on our shortcomings and imperfections.

After we discover what our insecurities are, and where they came from, we can then begin to build them into strengths. This can help lessen some of those awful feelings of Jealousy we might struggle with in regards to our GirlFriends. If we feel our life is lacking in certain areas, with God's help, we can begin making specific changes and choices which will lead us toward our desired goals.

So, What's a Girl to DO?

The antidote for low self-esteem is:

1. *Trace the source of your low self-esteem. Learn what you can from your past disappointments, and use it as preparation for your future.*

2. *Make a list of all things you like about yourself. Characteristics, physical attributes, talents, relationships, past accomplishments.*

3. *FOCUS on the positive. "Whatever is true, whatever is just, whatever is pure, whatever is lovely, whatever is commendable, if something is excellent or praiseworthy, think about these things." Philippians 4:8*

4. *Be Confident in Who Jesus says you are. You have everything you need to run the race God has set before you. Get into agreement with what He says about you.*

5. *Be Intentional. Remember, just wanting changes in your life doesn't change anything!*

Comparisons:

Competition is not always bad. Just as with any athletic or singing contest, it can make you perform at an even higher level than without it. There are also some GirlFriend relationships where a certain level of competition does exist and it can be healthy. I'm sure many of you have taken notice of that in your own life.

Then, there are those other times, a GirlFriends excels at a faster pace than you do in particular areas. Like how do you feel when your GirlFriend gets married and you want to be, buys a new house on the beach, lands the job you applied for, or drops 25 pounds in a week, and you can't seem to lose 2 pounds in a month? You're supposed to be happy for her, right? OK, GirlFriends, let me help you out here. The correct answer to this question will always be "*Right*"!

So, maybe it wasn't the very first thought you had when you heard the good news. But, it's not how you begin your thoughts that matters, it's what you DO with them afterwards that counts. Trust me, it's ok to admit those initial feelings were not very complimentary. Welcome to the human race, this side of heaven.

However, if you begin wishing and hoping your GirlFriend loses any of those things she has worked so hard to attain (or not), then Houston, we have a problem.

When we feel we are lacking something others have, it can open us up to being resentful towards those who are more fortunate than we are, either materially, socially, spiritually or physically. Your sense of self is constantly measuring itself up against your ideals and coming to various conclusions. If you measure up, you are *tickled pink, walking on air, or on cloud nine*. If you don't meet up to those standards, you may feel *down in the dumps, singing the blues,* or *in the pits* about yourself and your situation.

Such competition and comparison with others can then become the yardstick by which we measure ourselves. Since Envy is triggered when we come up short, we then tend to adjust the measurements in our minds by either tearing down our GirlFriends, elevating ourselves, or both. Teddy Roosevelt once said it well, "Comparison is the thief of JOY."

See, here is the problem. In the *Comparison Game*, there is always going to be a winner and a loser. Unfortunately for us, as life would have it, we will not always be the girl who receives the 'gold medal'. There will always be someone who is more talented, smarter, prettier, wiser, more popular, wealthier, has more GirlFriends, or whatever else.

I asked a group of women what their most difficult issue was in dealing with their GirlFriends. Their answer was *FOMO*. Being from a different generation, I had no idea what that meant. They said it's an acronym for Fear of Missing Out! Wow, who knew. It seemed pretty much everyone except me. Most of us want to be included, and accepted, so, I can understand why *FOMO*, or being uninvited to join in on the fun, would be a reason we would experience Jealousy or Envy with our GirlFriends.

A recent study found social media has added so much more fuel to this *What about Me* and *one-upping fire*. As I mentioned in a prior chapter, it has the potential to be the biggest culprit in regards to inciting these feelings of Jealousy and Envy among our GirlFriends. It makes complete sense as we witness the constant barrage of the happiest moments in people's lives on full display 24-7.

I warned you earlier, in Chapter 2, we would dig deeper into the use of social media. Here's where it gets a little rough, GirlFriends. This sometimes *contrived* world we are seeing, gives us the impression that everyone else's life is perfect and full of everything good, except ours. When we look at all the smiling faces of friends at parties, and the overwhelming amount of photos capturing the perfect family, on their perfect vacation, in the most perfect location in the world, it makes us believe we are missing out on all the best things life has to offer, but are we?

We need to be truly honest by asking ourselves *why* are we constantly posting all those photos? Is it to build ourselves up or to make our life look better than it really is? Is the message we are trying to relay: 'Look at me, see how significant I am, I have so many friends or I am so happy, too.' Do we purposely try to make others feel Jealous or Envious?

We seem to have gotten so caught up in this phenomenon, that we even begin comparing how many 'friends' our friends have and take notice of the number *tweets* that get *retweeted*! If we receive a lot, we feel pretty darn good about ourselves. IF we only get a few *thumbs up*, or none at all, we are devastated, and tell ourselves no one really *'likes'* or cares about us! Been there, done that? Ugh!

Are you mad at me yet? I'm sorry ~

I'm definitely not saying there is no place for these types of 'friends' in our lives or that all social media is evil. God certainly does use it for good, as we connect in positive ways to build up our GirlFriends, family, and even strangers across the city, and around the world. Neither am I saying it's not good to enjoy and share the blessings of God.

But, we live in a space now where there is so much 'clicking' and 'dinging' going on, it's almost as if we believe the one who has the most 'likes' and 'friends' wins something. So, what's the prize anyway? Does it make us feel any better about ourselves, or does it actually make us feel worse at times?

These are challenging times GirlFriends, and it takes much prayer and reflection to even get to the bottom of all of this. I'm sure the majority of us post because we want others to join in our happiness and excitement. But, are you aware not everyone needs or even wants to know every single thought, opinion, or activity going on in your life or mine?

I'm not going to lie to you. I know I don't particularly care to see every time a GirlFriend goes to the grocery store, gets a haircut, or is out to lunch with a friend other than me. As we have talked about before, in most of the *Games* we play, *motive* must always be the first thing we examine. The bible says in Galatians 1:10: "Obviously, I am not trying to win the approval of people, but of God. If pleasing people were my goal, I would not be Christ's servant."

In all those seemingly picture-perfect moments, (and most of them are) we need to keep in mind everything we own, and all the wonderful experiences we have are all gifts from God, and we are to be grateful to the Giver. The problem lies when we focus *mainly* on external things to make us happy, fulfilled and significant. We must live by the standard God has set before us as stated in 1Timothy 6:17 which says: "Instruct those who are rich in this present world not to be conceited or to fix their hope on the uncertainty of riches, but on God, who richly supplies us with all things to enjoy."

Whew, Ok, enough said! You survived and so did I! Good job!

So, What's a Girl to DO if your GirlFriend is Jealous of you?

You can help a GirlFriend overcome her Envy and Jealousy by:

(a) *Addressing her jealousy directly.*

(b) *Asking her how she is doing personally.*

(c) *Acknowledging things you like about her.*

(d) *Admitting you have struggles too.*

(e) *Accepting her into more group activities*

(f) *Assuring her the friendship is important to you.*

(g) *Emphasizing reasons you value spending time with her.*

(h) *Reassuring her you are not replacing her with other friends.*

(i) *Talking about your blessings may need to be done cautiously.*

Sometimes it might be difficult to decipher if we are Jealous or Envious of a GirlFriend? Perhaps we are in denial. Here are some telltale signs you might want to be aware of.

- *Withdraw from her*
- *Give Back-handed compliments*
- *Put her down*
- *Diminish her successes*
- *Super mean*
- *Overly competitive*
- *Not supportive*
- *Critique her appearance*
- *Guiltify her for her blessings*
- *Discourage her from moving forward*

To any of us who are on the viewing end of the camera, I have a few questions we can ask ourselves too: What is it about your GirlFriend, her vacations or joyful events that make you feel Envious or Jealous of her? It's easy to get caught up in *'the grass is always greener on the other side'* syndrome. But just remember, it could just be 'artificial turf' you're seeing!

It's more than likely we will be Jealous and Envious of our GirlFriends if we aren't happy with ourselves. The more content we are in the various aspects of our own lives like love, social life, hobbies, family, career, spiritual life, physical attributes, the less Envious and resentful we will feel towards our GirlFriends. I heard this statement which says: "Jealousy is what happens to us when we count someone else's blessing instead of our own!"

Anyway, I'm sure you get the *picture*!

Do you find yourself having any negative reactions to your GirlFriends advantages? What do you think the reason is?

_____

_____

So, What's a Girl to DO ..... IF You are Jealous or Envious?

1. *The antidote for Jealousy and Envy is GRATITUDE! Keep a daily Gratitude Journal. Be thankful for exactly who you are, and what you have in your life right now! "LEARN to be content in whatever situation we find ourselves in. Little or much." Philippians 4:11*

2. *Limit your time on social media. Be honest with yourself concerning the reasons you are Envious.*

3. *Do what you can to make improvements in your own life to make it the best it can be. Make a list of your successes, and your goals.*

4. *Don't Seek the approval of others, but rather God's.*

5. *Focus on your strengths. Post them somewhere visible, but NOT on social media!*

For some of us, dealing with these feelings of Jealousy and Envy can be a constant battle. We need to resist the temptation to play the *Comparison Game* with anyone else knowing that there is no one else in the world exactly like you. You can feel secure in the fact that God has equipped you with everything you *need* right now in order to be all He has called *you* to be!

We must choose *daily* to be in control of those urges by doing what my awesome grandkids did when confronted with this 'green-eyed monster': Be happy for your GirlFriends, Express it with your Words, and be Grateful for all you *Do* have!

Wearing green may be fashionable for St. Patrick's Day or even Christmas, but *'seeing green'* is definitely not a message we want to communicate to our GirlFriends. As Christ followers, Envy and Jealousy will never be in style no matter what season of the year it is!

We Pretend to Be

Who We Are Not,

Because

We are Afraid

of Being Rejected,

For Who

We Are!

CHAPTER 7
What About Me?

"He was Despised and Rejected by Men."

Isaiah 53:3

News flash! *NOT* everyone is going to like you, or me either, no matter how wonderful we are, or how much we try to make them! I know it's difficult for us to accept that fact sometimes, but it really is impossible to go through life without feeling the sting of Rejection. Abraham Lincoln had it right when he said: *"You can please some of the people some of the time, all of the people some of the time, but you can never please ALL of the people ALL of the time."* And that's the truth!

We all have an innate, fundamental, need to belong, be valued and accepted, but unfortunately, Rejection does the complete opposite of that. It's one of the most common emotional wounds we will receive in our daily lives. Oh, we do our absolute best to be the most dedicated woman, boss, sister, wife, neighbor, mother and GirlFriend possible.

That's exactly the reason it catches us so off guard when it happens to us. It doesn't matter whether it's simply not getting invited to a party, being turned down for your dream job or being stood up for a date. Those feelings of being *cast aside* can show up at any time, and through anyone.

However, when it comes at the hands of a GirlFriend, it hurts even more, and the closer the friendship, the more intense the pain. Now that we are all depressed, myself included, what is Rejection? Not that we need a formal definition, but I'm going to give it to you anyway. It's what I do. Hang in there, GirlFriends, because in this chapter we will Identify what Rejection looks like, Discuss how it affects us, and of course, Examine what the *rules* are in winning at this debilitating *Game*.

DEFINITION of REJECTION:

Webster calls it: *A refusal to accept or consider something or someone. It implies sending or throwing away, discarding, ignoring, snubbing, excluding, shutting out, avoiding someone or something.*

As I looked further into the synonyms for this word, it sent chills up and down my spine! Brrr!

Synonyms for Rejection are:

Cold shoulder (maybe that's why!) Kicked in the teeth, Slapped in the Face, Brushed-off, Dismissed, and Turned down!

It's no wonder we feel so dejected after getting Rejected! I realize this next story is not about GirlFriend relationships per se. However, it shows us how Rejection can not only affect us at the time it occurred, but how it can also influence us for many years to come, *IF* we allow it to.

I can remember experiencing almost all the above feelings after returning home from one of those weekly, Saturday night high school dances. Some of you know what I'm talking about. Those places were like cesspools of Rejection, just waiting to happen. My GirlFriends and I would have fun early in the evening, while we were doing all the fast dances together. You know, the Stroll, the Monkey, and the Twist. Well, if you don't know what I'm talking about, YouTube it! I would typically try to quickly *waltz* out of the building just before the last song of the evening was played. It was always that you know what: the slow, 'Boy's Choice' dance.

These guys would scout the room out, looking for the cutest girl there, or at least one they thought might be willing to dance with them. Just the thoughts of that scene still freak me out! Now that I think about it, I feel more sorry for all the Rejection those poor boys must have endured, than I do for myself right now. I'm sure there are others of you GirlFriends who attended those dances who have had similar self-esteem issues, as well!

I spent way too many evenings hopelessly waiting to be selected. The battle cry in my heart was always the same. '*Look at Me, Pick Me, Choose Me, Pleeease!*' It's pitiful to even say this, but at some point, I realized I didn't even care who the boy was. The only thing that mattered at the time, was someone acknowledging me, and making me feel as if I were good enough to be chosen. Sad to say, it seldom happened.

So, week after week, Rejection upon Rejection, in order to protect what little self esteem I had left, I began making excuses for why I couldn't attend anymore. It was one of the only times I can remember being happy I had three little brothers I could say I needed to stay home to babysit. Of course, I didn't do that, but my GirlFriends didn't know. I guess they do now!

That was the core message I kept hearing over and over again. Avoiding, Shunning, Excluding, REJECTING! Why didn't these boys like me, was I honestly that unlovable? Perhaps it was the Annette Funicello frizzy, permed, 'poodle' hairstyle I had. Maybe it was the thick, coke bottle, white, cat-eye glasses I wore. There was a saying made famous years ago by Dorothy Parker, which said *"Boys don't make passes at girls who wear glasses!"*

I think that may have been true in those days. Fortunately, today glasses have become more of a trendy, fashion statement instead. Wearing them bothered me so much, guess what I purchased when I cashed my very first paycheck? You got it, contact lenses. I was willing to spend $300 for one pair of *killer*, hard, plastic lenses that made my eyes red, watery and sore. That was a lot of money in those days and pain as well, but oh, so worth it.

Not only did it change how I felt about myself, but the boys seemed to like me a little more too! "Man *does* look on the outside, but God looks at the heart."1 Samuel 16:7 Those awful, constant feelings of not measuring up in other people's *eyes* made me struggle with the *What's Wrong with Me Game*, well into my adult years.

Feeling or being Rejected only seems to confirm some of the things we may already believe, or not like about ourselves. So, just when our self-esteem is already hurting the most, we go ahead and damage it a little more by our own unfavorable self talk. When faced with a Rejection, the voices in our own heads are discouraging us by saying things like: 'I'm ugly', 'Nothing ever goes right for me', 'I'm such a loser', and the list goes on.

I hope you realize, during these times, there is an enemy out there, and his '*soul*' purpose is "To steal, kill, and destroy" you and to keep anything good from coming into your life. He knows we are probably not going to get involved in the *big* sins of the world, but as long as he can keep us focused on the Rejection itself, and doubt ourselves and the goodness of God, he is the biggest winner in this *Disapproval Game*. But remember what the last portion of that verse says, though. Jesus said: "I have come that you might have life, and have it to the fullest." John 10:10 Thank you, Jesus!

So, What's a Girl to DO?

As natural as it might seem for us to want to list all our own faults after being Rejected, resist the temptation and encourage yourself with God's Words instead. When you are feeling left out or ignored, next time instead of focusing on a 'What's *wrong* with me?' attitude, get into the habit of turning it around by saying: 'What is *RIGHT* with me?' Philippians 4:8-9 instructs us to meditate on: "Whatever is right, whatever is pure, whatever is lovely, whatever is admirable, if anything is excellent or praiseworthy, think about such things ~ and the peace of God will be with you."

It's not being 'pride-full' to encourage yourself; it's being 'mind-full' of the truth of who God says you are. Go out and purchase the prettiest journal you can find, along with a beautifully embellished pen, then fill it to the brim with His Words of affirmation. Write down all the wonderful things about yourself, and the amazing blessings you have had in your life!

Whenever you begin to doubt or put yourself down, open the pages of your book, and read out loud everything you can be grateful for. Let me know how that works out for you! Henri J.M. Nouwen is quoted as saying: *"Self-Rejection is the greatest enemy of the spiritual life, because it contradicts the sacred voice that calls us the Beloved.*

Oh, how I wish I could go back, especially to those teenage years, and take my own advice, and know the truth of who I really was. Since I can't do that, when those feelings of Rejection attack me even now, I do what I am encouraging you to do by reminding myself of God's promises concerning the truths of who I am in Christ.

So, What's a Girl to DO?

Recall a time when a Rejection was so strong, it still affects you now.

Have you learned how to apply God's Words to your life when you feel Rejected? List some of those truths God says about you.

Many of us handle Rejection by consistently giving in to the *Compliance Game.* It's pretty much what I did, by rushing out to purchase contact lenses in order to feel good about myself. At times, we will do whatever it takes to keep from being ridiculed or unaccepted again. Giving into peer pressure fits into the pattern of always 'bending over backwards' or 'twisting ourselves into a pretzel' to *GET* others to like us.

If we never get to the place of understanding why we respond like we do in certain situations, or what our underlying motives are for doing things, we will always live with a performance-based identity. It says: '*IF* I do this, then I'll get that.' You will constantly be 'jumping through all the right hoops' in order to obtain someone else's approval.

There is absolutely nothing wrong with self improvement or looking our best. I always say, "*If the barn needs painting ~ paint it!*" I also believe as *God's Girls*, we *do* need to present ourselves to others even better than the *world* does, as a testimony of His goodness to us. On the other hand, concentrating on our exterior

ONLY is not a suitable substitute for being an inwardly confident and godly woman.

Rejection isn't only about the emotional feelings we get at the time an event happens. It's the deeper message we receive which speaks to the heart of who we are, and causes us to believe the lies about ourselves. It's not just our imagination either which causes us to feel bad about ourselves. Psychologists tell us we can relive and re-experience emotional pain more vividly than we can the physical pain.

Try recalling, right now, a situation in which you felt significant, physical pain, perhaps a migraine, or how about labor pains. Now, *STOP.* So, how does that make you feel? Nothing! You remember it, but your brain's pathways will not even respond to it. You can't *feel* that exact same pain you did then, you just remember it hurt. In other words, the memory alone won't give you physical pain.

Now, try imagining a painful Rejection from a GirlFriend or a situation which hurt you deeply. Actually, don't do that, just take my word for it! You *will* be flooded with many of the *same* emotions you had at the time. Your brain will respond much as it did when it occurred. It's called *Emotional Memory.*

Every time we retell a sad or hurtful story, or replay in our own mind, we will probably still experience similar emotions from it. That's the reason we need to, at the appropriate time, stop repeating those distressing events over and over. We must take our Rejection to the *ONLY* Person who can truly free us from the pain of it. "He is near to the brokenhearted, and rescues the crushed in spirit." Psalms 34:18

Neuroscience tells us that even *perceived* Rejection activates the same part of the brain as where we experience physical pain, like a punch in the stomach. OUCH! So, when we say it hurts so bad, we really mean it, literally! It doesn't matter if it's true or not. Just *thinking* you have been *cast aside* tells your mind the same thing! So much so, that taking pain medicine can help alleviate the emotional pain. That's pretty amazing, don't you think?

A great deal of human emotions arise in response to real, anticipated, remembered, or even imagined Rejection by others. It causes us to pull away from others and increases our sadness, loneliness, jealousy, guilt, shame, and depression. In fact, much of the hurt and struggles we experience are not even based on the Rejection itself, but rather on what we tell ourselves about the event!

We all know what it feels like being *dismissed*, but healthy people see Rejection as a normal occurrence in life. They don't let it define who they really are. They are able to look at it as an incident that took place, learn from it, then they are able to move forward in a shorter period of time.

It's not that they don't feel bad or struggle getting through a hurt, it's that they don't allow it to overshadow the entire view of their day or life. If we have a healthy self image, it means we can still recognize all the other blessings we have in our lives, despite a Rejection.

Unhealthy GirlFriends don't see the entire picture; they only see it as it's all about them. They are all consumed with the negative emotions they are feeling from the harsh words, or situations. They allow remnants of old Rejections to escalate, causing them to overreact in future situations. Rejection has a way of destroying a person's life in a way that few other things can, *if* we let it.

Would you say you handle rejections in a healthy or unhealthy manner?

Let's do another little self examination. I don't want to put any added pressure on you to perform, but if you don't admit it, you can't change it! We all handle Rejection, or the fear of it differently. Here are some methods we might use when we're trying to be accepted. Circle the ones you practice in your life.

- **Performer**: *She overcompensates for her low self-esteem, in the hopes she will be liked. She attempts to be funny, entertaining, and the life of the party. She's the hostess with the mostest, a Martha Stewart type.*

- **Clinger**: *She attaches herself to others to boost her lack of confidence. She craves being with her GirlFriends all the time, and needs lots of validation and approval. She's too accommodating, giving more than she gets.*

- **Controller**: *She is co-dependent, and feels responsible to take care of everyone else's feelings, needs and problems, sometimes ahead of hers. She's a "Do what I say, because I know what's best for you, kind of girl."*

- **Winner**: *She is ALWAYS right. She has a difficult time receiving constructive criticism. She has an angry need to prove herself. She will argue until she is blue in the face.*

- **Defendant:** *She'll cut herself off from others, especially IF she might be viewed in a negative light. She shies away from life's challenges, so as not to fail. She protects herself from future humiliations and shame.*

- **'Correct-oid':** *She is opinionated, will always inform you about something, even if she has little understanding of it herself. A know-it-all. She corrects you if you say or do anything wrong, according to her.*

- **Fixer:** *She's eager to tell everyone how to change their life. This GirlFriend attempts to be your Holy Spirit. She loves when her GirlFriends come to her for advice.*

- **Downer:** *She always takes a pessimistic attitude and finds the worst-case scenario in every situation. She will constantly tell you all the negative reasons you shouldn't do something, buy something, or go somewhere.*

- **Checker:** *FOMO: The Fear of Missing Out GirlFriend! She's constantly checking her phone to see everything her GirlFriends are doing. Do they look better than her, have more friends or are they having more fun!*

How was that? Did you see yourself in any of the descriptions? When we feel crushed from a painful Rejection, thinking clearly is not quite as simple as you might think. I'm going to confess to you a time which was agonizing for me when several of my GirlFriends Rejected me, big time. I am very happy they didn't have social media in those days or I might still be in therapy!

That's exactly how I felt - crushed and bruised - when I was *NOT* asked by four of my closest GirlFriends to attend a girls' weekend of out of town shopping. Yes, you heard it correctly, I did say my *CLOSEST* friends! To add fuel to the fire, when I innocently called 'Gail' (no cell phones at the time) to talk about an upcoming women's event we were overseeing, her husband informed me she was not at home. The problem began with his announcement that he was not *allowed* to tell me where she was, nor who she was with! However, after hearing my whimpering, he quickly *'spilled the beans'* about exactly where she went and he even named all who went with her! Aww, such a 'softy'.

I played those awful words over and over again in my mind. Exactly what I am telling you not to do. The thoughts that they had met together in secret, planned this trip, then made a decision to purposefully leave me out. What terrible thing had I said or done to deserve this deliberate, Rejection? Obviously, they had every right to go anywhere with whoever they chose, and do anything they wanted without me or my permission. However, I still felt betrayed, left out, hurt, confused, and *MAD*!

So, after hanging up with 'Gail's' husband, I did what any good Christian girl would do. I went right over to their houses and 'toilet-papered' them all! Take it easy GirlFriends, I'm just kidding. I threw a lovely *'What's wrong with me party'*, of which I was the only one who attended. Although, my husband *did* show up after my 'wailing' permeated the entire house. I guess he figured something must have been *up* with me!

I gave him the *long* version of the story, which he knew was in his *best* interest to listen attentively to. Naturally, he sympathized with me. Honestly, he didn't even take my side (which annoyed me). He simply said in his typical calming voice that he could understand how I could *feel* that way. Did I mention he has a Masters Degree in Counseling? Comes in handy with me around.

Another little side-note here ~

Please be careful who you share your struggles and disappointments with. Sometimes what happens is, you work through them, then get over them. The problem is, in many cases, the person you told.....doesn't! They take up the offense for you, then may harbor a grudge against your GirlFriend because she hurt you. This is especially true when it comes to husband and wife situations. You have an argument, you make up, are all lovey dovey, and your Mother is still furious with your husband. Understood?

Getting back to the shoppers ~

I will, in this case, not tell you what my 'flesh' said to do. Ok, I guess I will. I first prayed to God that they would have a miserable time while away, and they would feel as guilty as sin for excluding me! They didn't. Either one. I considered *calling them out* at the ladies' event that weekend. Hey, I had the microphone, and I was the MC.

I wanted to go tell all my other GirlFriends what they had done to me too so they would feel sorry for me, and tell me how I didn't deserve that. I am such a nice person, aren't I? Don't answer that question! Well, obviously, as you can see, I wasn't thinking or behaving very nice right then. However, I'm thankful I didn't act out on any of my awful thoughts or feelings.

But, that's how Rejection *can* cause us to *FEEL*, especially when we don't respond to the *Being Left Out Game*, God's way. We will want to, and unfortunately at times, strike back by returning evil for evil. Two can play this *Game*, right? Absolutely, wrong! The *Good News* is we don't need to give in to everything our emotions tell us to do. We have a choice. Romans 8:9 reminds us: "You are not controlled by your sinful nature. You are controlled by the Holy Spirit if you have the Spirit of God living in you."

That's exactly what I chose to do. I poured my heart out to God, and told Him how I was honestly feeling. I asked Him to forgive me for my desires to hurt them for hurting me. I also asked Him to help me to forgive them, and change my attitude toward them. I wanted to be in a good place before speaking with' Gail' about the situation.

When they returned from their shopping excursion, I called 'Gail' to express how disappointed I was that I was not invited to go, and probably even more upset how they intentionally kept it hush-hush. I simply asked her why. I wanted to know IF maybe they were *mad at me* for something I had said or done previously. I thought that was a fair enough question to ask, don't you?

To my total astonishment she became so enraged at my even *questioning* her decision to go without me. She stated it was none of my business, and other things I will not repeat to you. I informed her I was not going to listen to her rant at me, but would be happy to discuss the situation when she was calmer. Then, she hung up on me! I guess she hasn't calmed down yet, because even after all these years later, I have never heard a single word from her again! I mean like ever.

I'm not going to say dealing with the ongoing remnants of this circumstance was easy. It definitely was not. What made this situation even more difficult, besides being together at the women's event that weekend, was we were all a part of the same circle of GirlFriends. I constantly had to deal with the fake smiles, and cordial pleasantries, when we crossed paths. Awkward!

To be honest, it was a struggle at times to keep what happened to myself. It took all my strength, and the Lord's, to resist the urge to explain to our other GirlFriends my side of the story. I'm not sure what her version was or who she told, if anyone. I just know I never did!

The process of working through this 'falling out' took me a very long time to get through. Eventually, I was able to let it go, and not hold it against her. Rejection hurts, especially when there is no explanation, and it comes from some of your best friends. Outwardly smiling, but inwardly *'smarting'* from this experience, made me withdraw to my safe space, in order to protect myself from even more damage, or from possibly affecting someone else.

I thought of quitting all the women's activities or going to another church altogether, but my husband was one of the pastors on staff, so it left that option out! I just slowly began to stop trusting others with my whole heart.

You know what they say: "With friends like that, who needs enemies." But, my dear Sisters, when we become Christ's followers, we don't have the luxury anymore of giving into those kinds of *Games* GirlFriends play. 2 Corinthians 5:17 states when we surrender our life to Christ, "Old things pass away, ALL things must become new." That means our former ways of thinking, speaking, acting and responding.

As you can see, being a pastor's wife or even after walking with the Lord for many years, doesn't shield us from the sting of Rejection. It still hurts just as deeply. Two of my other GirlFriends who went on that trip, called me a couple days after returning to apologize. They said they knew something didn't *feel* right that weekend. They never told me what happened, and I didn't ask. I forgave them immediately, and we didn't skip a beat in our friendship, because of their quick and sincere apology.

After a GirlFriend Rejects you, your *history* alone may not be enough to hold your friendship together. I'm sorry to say, in some situations, it may never return to the way it was before. It doesn't mean that you are worthless or unlovable, or even that she is. Maybe she had a bad day or made a poor decision which affected you. Perhaps she misunderstood something you said or did. This was a time I knew only God could fix my broken heart because it was impossible for me to do so!

Even though we never spoke again, I still extended God's grace and forgiveness to 'Gail'. It's not because of who she is or because I'm such a wonderful person. I did it because of

Whose I am. My life has been paid for at a tremendous cost, and so has hers; by Jesus Christ Himself. I don't ever want to disappoint Him or compromise my relationship with Him because of the carelessness of a friend or because of my own hurt feelings. The bible says, IF we don't forgive others, God will not forgive us. We will examine this subject extensively in Chapter 9.

My story is not so different from many of yours. I knew *MY* responsibility was to forgive, and to be available for the possibility of restoring the relationship. As I look back in hindsight, could I have done anything different? Sure, there are a few things I might have changed.

The first thing is perhaps I would not have given up so easily on our friendship. It's my tendency and weakness, as I said before, to run away when I feel beaten up or Rejected. I could have *pushed through* the situation by stopping by her house with some fresh baked cookies, flowers, or whatever. Maybe I also could have put aside my stubborn declaration of '*When SHE is ready, SHE will call me*'.

Unfortunately, I chose not to do any of those things, for fear of her anger, or even more so, of her Rejection of me again. I guess I will never know how it may have turned out had I decided to go the extra mile. I couldn't do anything to change what happened, so I made peace with my decision, gained much wisdom from that test, and moved forward with a grateful heart for all the wonderful memories we shared.

We have all experienced at one time or another, the sting of Rejection caused by a GirlFriend. It wasn't the first time, and it certainly will not be my last one either. I continue to adjust my attitudes and reactions to line up with God's will for me the next time I feel Rejected, because there WILL be a next time.

We've heard 'time heals all wounds', and that is true. However, I can't overstate enough how dealing with the scars of Rejection, is a process. It takes time, and time, and sometimes even more time to repair our heart from this kind of *Exclusion Game*.

So, What's a Girl to DO?

Here are some healthy ways we can learn to cooperate with God in the healing process.

Give up. *your way of reacting, and practice God's way of handling Rejection.*

Open up. *Be honest with yourself about how you feel. Don't withdraw to protect yourself. Don't stop trusting your GirlFriends with your heart.*

Look up. *When you're going through something difficult and you wonder where God is, remember the teacher is always quiet during the test.*

Listen up. *Read and meditate on God's Word. Focus on the truths about who you really are, not what the world or your GirlFriends say about you. SEEK to understand where she is coming from.*

Grow up. *Self Rejection is another piece to this puzzle. Rebuild your self-esteem when it happens. Affirm valuable aspects of yourself.*

Lighten up. *Don't take everything others say too personal. Keep things in perspective. It's not who you are, it's just something that happened to you.*

Fess up. *Re-evaluate possible blind spots you could improve on. Do similar scenarios come up often? What did you learn, and what can you do better next time?*

Are you still carrying around the wounds of a Rejection from years past? With who? What steps can you take to begin the healing process?

_____

_____

We know what Rejection is: The refusal to be accepted or valued.

We know what it Feels like: Sad, Mad, Worthless, Unlovable, Punched In The Gut!

We know how it Affects us: Withdrawing, Low Self Esteem, Overcompensating.

Just as Jesus' Rejection did not get to have the final say in His Life, being Rejected by a GirlFriend doesn't need to get the last word in our lives either, unless *WE* say it does!

As Long as

Everything Goes

Exactly the Way

I Want,

I Can Be

Totally Flexible!

CHAPTER 8
You Don't Own Me!

"Love is not arrogant or rude. It does not insist on its own way."

1 Corinthians. 13:5

Ok, sing along with me now. *"You Don't Own Me*, don't try to change me in any way. Don't tell me what to do, and don't tell me what to say, just let me be myself, that's all I ask of you."* Very good! Even though there's a new *rap* version of this song, I still prefer the original, first sung in 1963 by Lesley Gore. Of course, I was just a baby back then. But no matter which rendition you prefer, the question still remains the same: Who really wants to be owned or Controlled by another human being?

I know I sure don't, and I think I can safely say you don't either. I have 'pushed back' in my own life on occasion, when my husband had asked me to do something I wasn't particularly fond of. I have enthusiastically sung at the top of my lungs my own version of that song. For some unknown reason, it always seems to make me feel a little *freer* afterwards! Now, I will say in my husband's defense, he is definitely not a Control Freak. That's mainly because I would never *let* him be!

So, I purposefully kept this *My Way or the Highway* for the last *Game* because I thought I didn't have much to say on the topic. However, by the time I completed penning this chapter,

I discovered I wrote this one for ~ *ME*! Just a warning, you may want to enter this one at your own risk.

Part of the problem with this *Game* is many of us don't see ourselves as Controlling people, especially when we believe we know what's best for our GirlFriends. Isn't it our obligation then to let them know the right way of doing things, especially when we know what that way is?

We wonder what's so wrong with simply trying to *help* our GirlFriends out by giving them our opinion. Nothing *is* wrong with it, *IF* of course, they want or ask for it! Seriously, it *is* difficult sometimes to know how much input we *should* have in other people's lives. What is our responsibility and what is not?

Stick around, as we explore those answers and these: What is Control, Are you a Control Freak, What's the difference between Healthy Control and Over Control, and Does God have a remedy for the Controller?

DEFINITION of CONTROL:

Dictionary.com says it is *"The act or power of controlling, regulating, dominating or commanding."*

Webster states it is: *"To have power over, rule, have direct influence over, authority to guide or manage. Supervise, govern, and boss"*.

Ok, so is all control bad? Absolutely not! There are times we *must* manage people and situations in our lives. IF you're the boss, a teacher, or a mom, you *do* need to oversee your work environment, your classroom, or your household. To do otherwise would be irresponsible.

Certainly, no mom would ever allow her 10-year-old to take a test drive on the interstate with her brand-new Mercedes convertible now, would she? (Dream on) Perhaps some Dads might, but we'll save that discussion for someone else's book! Being in the *driver's seat* can be a positive thing, unless of course, it's not your car or you're the *back seat* passenger.

Speaking of Moms: while growing up, my Mother often tried to teach my sister Jeanne and I how to wash, fold, and iron clothes the *proper* way. Does anyone else still iron, besides me? We were also trained the *correct* way of washing and waxing floors, washing and drying dishes by hand, and packing her Stanley Home Product orders. With my mother working several jobs, we were assigned plenty of work to keep us busy. Too much, I always said. Now you understand why I sing the *You Don't Own Me* song!

It didn't take her very long to figure out I was never going to be a Rachael Ray in the kitchen, though. I think she came to that conclusion shortly after the eggs I was *supposed* to be watching boil, exploded all over the walls, ceiling, and stove. Have you ever smelled rotten eggs? We did ~ for weeks! Shortly after that incident, she stopped allowing me in the kitchen, except to eat and do dishes. That's when we learned the important message of: *"IF you want something done right, you gotta do it yourself"!* I was hoping she would follow through on that philosophy with *ALL* the chores. She didn't!

As a child, what I heard her saying was the job I was doing did not meet up to her expectations. Trust me when I say, my mother was not a Control Freak, by any means. Generally speaking, Control Freaks have a difficult time letting go of people, situations, and power. They seldom delegate anything for others to do, and *IF* they do, they will typically micromanage them. I can testify to the fact she definitely did *NOT* have a problem letting go of housework. Being widowed at 36 years young, and left with the responsibility of raising 6 young children, she honestly was in survival mode.

Control Girls, though, believe there is only one right way of doing just about everything, and they seem to be the only ones who know what that is! They don't have any problem telling you their way either. My husband has a great philosophy when it comes to *helping* others, especially as it relates to adult children. He says it's usually best to refrain from giving our *unsolicited or unasked for* advice and opinions, but instead, wait to be an *Invited Consultant*. Wow, is he good? This was a key discovery in my path to letting go of my inclination to be a Control Freak.

As in my Mother's case, taking control, and striving for excellence are not negative in themselves. Most successful people don't live their lives in a haphazard or flippant way. Like whatever happens, happens. Because we've been given the Spirit of self-control, we need to make every effort to have discipline in many areas of our lives:

- *Our Emotions*: *Controlling our Feelings*
- *Our Time*: *Using it Wisely*
- *Our Thoughts*: *Taking them Captive*
- *Our Actions*: *Doing what's Right*
- *Our Decisions*: *Weighing all things Carefully*
- *Our Friends*: *Choosing them Wisely*
- *Our Children*: *Raising them in a Godly manner*
- *Our Finances*: *Spending it Responsibly*
- *Our Body*: *Glorifying God*
- *Our Home*: *Keeping it orderly*

I'm exhausted just looking over this list. Is it okay then to Control whatever we want as long as it's about us and our own activities? Sure, as long as we're not being obsessive/compulsive concerning it. Master Controllers put their energies in all the wrong places. Everyone else's business! If they would focus on cultivating each of these areas listed above, they wouldn't have enough time, let alone energy, to take charge of other people's lives!

Now, let's investigate a little more what a true Control Freak looks like. I think this may be where the problem lies.

DEFINITION of a CONTROL FREAK:

The Learner's Dictionary describes it as: A term first used in 1970, it's *"A person who has a strong NEED to control people, or how things are done."* Google says*: "A person who feels an obsessive need to exercise control over themselves and others, and to take command of every situation."*

That pretty much says it all. The difference between a person who is *in* control and a *Control Freak* is motivation and method. She has a strong or obsessive *NEED* to Control everyone and every situation in her life and her GirlFriends' lives too. Know anyone like that? Perhaps someone near and dear to you? Could *YOU* possibly be that person?

You know, *Control Freaks* rarely admit, or even realize they are doing anything wrong. They seldom see themselves as manipulators, and they can't seem to understand how others see things differently than they do. One of the many downsides of this girl's method is she stifles the ability of others to grow, flourish, or even think for themselves while playing this *Game*.

It's difficult for them to know when they're crossing the line from being a good influence with their GirlFriends, to trying to *get them* to do, say, or think the way they themselves do. Here's a little test to see IF you perhaps have gone over to the negative side of Control. Now worries, I won't score you on this one!

Dr. Karl Albrecht Ph.D, has allowed me to utilize and adapt this quiz to measure the level of your Control Thermometer. He says, *"Although not scientifically perfect, and probably not psychologically complete, it can give you a quick perspective on your own Control-seeking tendencies".*

For each question, choose a number on a one through five-point scale that best describes you.

1 - Almost Never 2 - Seldom 3 - Sometimes
4 – Often 5 - Very Often.

Add up all 10 scores then consult the scale at the end.

Note: Even-numbered questions indicate personal control, and odd-numbered ones indicate control over others.

Be as honest as you can. As you answer each question, imagine someone who knows you well is looking over your shoulder. What would they say, and would they agree with your self-perception? Now, I'm not trying to Control your answers, just keeping you honest. Is that the same as 'womanipulation'? I made up the word! What do you think?

The Control Freak Quiz

1. Do you *help* others drive, telling them what route to take, when to turn, where to park, remind them that the traffic light has changed, when to break it?

2. Do you devote a lot of attention and energy to keeping your personal environment organized?

3. Do you give people a lot of *shoulds* and *oughts*, unsolicited advice, suggestions, or constructive criticism? Really think about this one!

4. Do you have lots of personal rules, routines, rituals, and ceremonies?

5. Are you the one who takes over and orders other people around, when the situation seems confused?

6. Do you dislike depending on others, accepting help from them, or allowing them to do things for you?

7. Do you insist on being right, having things done your way, or having the final word?

8. Do you over-plan simple activities?

9. Do you find it difficult to admit making mistakes, being wrong or misinformed about something, or acknowledge that you've changed your mind?

10. Do you become angry, irritable, or anxious when someone or something makes you late, when things don't start on time, or things don't go according to plan?

Interpret Your Score:

41 - 50 Yep, you're a Control freak.

31 – 40 You probably have some Control issues.

21 - 30 You can live and let live.

10 - 20 Are you really being honest? Haaaa!

Now, wasn't that *FUN*? Were you surprised by your results? I know I was. I didn't even think I had any issues in this area until

I took this quiz. One more area in my life for God to transform. This assessment offers us just one tool to help us evaluate our understanding of Control.

What did you learn about yourself?

_____

So, why do we attempt to Control others or their situations? Without psychoanalyzing our GirlFriends or ourselves too much, there are some universal explanations for this. Number one reason is because we lack Control in one or more areas of our *own* life. Because our brain always seeks the shortest path to attain a goal, we will try to *help* others with their *issues*, rather than taking care of our own. It's called *Creative Avoidance*. In other words, it's easier to tell someone else what to do to change, than to change ourselves! Oh, sister!

There's another sneaky factor which can turn a GirlFriend into a *Control Freak*. Needing to have authority over others, can be linked to a low self-esteem. It makes up for our lack of confidence and causes us to feel superior when giving others *constructive* criticism or advice.

Dominators also have a fear of letting go because of what *may* have happened to them in their past. At some point, they themselves may have been restrained, restricted or ruled over, which would lead them to try to take charge of everything in their present environment.

Do you remember when I mentioned in a prior chapter that we would revisit the topic of expectations again? Well, I am a woman of my word, so here it goes.

The *Control Freak* is most likely to be the one to set the rules and expectations for her GirlFriends, she then uses them to *get* her desired results. She consistently disapproves of how others do everything, even if her GirlFriends are trying to do things her way. She will do whatever it takes to *get* others to comply with those *rules* she has set up in her own mind for them.

Unfortunately, their GirlFriends don't always know what those rules are, because typically they're unspoken. Now, that's a real problem. Most of us seldom, if ever, verbally communicate those expectations. Sometimes, it's because we think the other person *should* already know them. I'm sorry to say, it doesn't work that way.

I'm sure you're surprised, but I have another story! ~

I discovered this when a GirlFriend called me recently, but I missed her call. Her voice mail message was pretty generic. It simply said: *"Hey, it's me, just checking in."* That was it. I didn't think twice about it, as I got caught up in the business of life for a couple days. When she called back, she snapped at me and said: *"Hey, I called you! Didn't you get my message?"* I said I had.

She said: *"Uh, then, why didn't you call me back?"* I said *"You didn't ask me to, and it didn't seem like it was anything important. IF it were, you would have asked me to call you."* She replied with a sigh, followed up by: *"Welllll, don't you know when someone calls you, you are 'supposed' to call them back!"* Wow, ok then, I did *NOT* get that memo, I thought to myself.

My mind went directly to Proverbs 15:1, which says, "A soft answer turns away wrath, but harsh words still up quarrels." So, I decided to make light of her *rule* by saying: *"Where exactly are those instructions located?"* We laughed about it, because I chose not to be defensive. Guess what?

Because now I knew her expectations in that area, I was willing and able to fulfill her request! The next time I miss her call, I will be sure to call her back. If it would not have been acceptable for me to comply, we would have needed to talk about it at some point.

What if she hadn't told me how she felt concerning my not calling her back, and buried it inside herself instead? Or, how do you think it would have *played out* had I overreacted to her *should have* remark, and taken up an offense? I would surmise, a whole lot different. She might have become *mad at me*. Perhaps she would have added it to her secret *bag* of unmet expectations, of which I had no idea was being filled up. If it continued, it could not only have hindered the authenticity of our friendship, but it may have eventually ended it.

Here's the thing. Her wanting me to call her back or whatever the issues are we have with a GirlFriend, need to be communicated as an 'expressed desire', or a 'humble request'. It's not fair to have unspoken *rules* for your GirlFriend to guess, or unrealistic expectations she *needs* to follow. When conversations go from a 'it would be my preference' to a 'you should have', then we have a Controlling mindset, which is totally unacceptable in a loving friendship or with God!

So, What's a Girl to DO?

How could you handle this situation differently if you were the caller? IF you don't get a returned call, instead of being offended, *you* can simply call your GirlFriend back! It honestly is not a big deal, unless we make it one. What was the real problem? She wanted to talk, right? This *Expectation Game* can be a real friendship breaker on so many levels, if played on an ongoing basis. Let's uncover some better ways of dealing with these types of situations.

*Communicate your desire to your GirlFriend, not expecting anything, except to be heard.

*Don't try to get your way through intimidation or forcing your ways on her. Instead say, "*I would really appreciate it IF you would...*" rather than you '*should have.*'

*Keep the problem, the problem, don't create a new one by being offended or Controlling.

*Don't take it personally. She didn't do anything to intentionally hurt you.

*Don't make mountains out of molehills. Have perspective!

*No put downs or making her feel bad because her ideas and preferences are different than yours.

*Take into account your GirlFriend's thoughts and feelings. Your way is not *always* the right way for everyone else.

Control Freaks will often put an unachievable or unknown expectation on their GirlFriends. They will sanction anyone who doesn't live up to their personal 'code of conduct' by criticizing or condemning anyone who doesn't agree with them. The underlying drive of Controllers is their desire to impose their will and agenda on you! There are different ways of doing this, but her end result is always the same. Ultimately, she just wants you to do things *her* way!

If her conditions to comply are met with any resistance, she may give you an unapproving *look* or withhold her love and support. She might even end the friendship if you habitually don't meet up to her expectations. Most *Control Freaks* have trouble maintaining meaningful and lasting relationships because of these sometimes subtle, yet domineering, tactics they use.

While there might be a variety of reasons why GirlFriends Control, they will use whatever pressure 'go-to modes' of relating simply because exerting power over someone else actually makes them feel good, at the time. As bizarre as it may seem, studies show *Control Freaks* experience the same satisfying feelings they receive when accomplishing something big or completing a job well done! It's like a fist pump in the air, followed by a "*YES!*"

So, What's a Girl to DO?

God's Word has the perfect solution for keeping your Controlling behavior from Controlling others. Galatians 5:16 tells us if we "Walk by the Spirit, and we will not carry out the desires of the flesh." As we continue on to verses 19-21, it lists the characteristics of being Controlled by our own selfish desires. Verses 22-24 describe the qualities exhibited *if* we allow the Holy Spirit to Control us. *YOU* get to choose.

FLESH	*SPIRIT*
Control Freak	*Self-Control*
Hold On	*Let Go*
Condemnation	*Acceptance*
Unrealistic Expectations	*Humble Desires*
Demands	*Requests*
'Womanipulation'	*Freedom*

Now, perhaps you breathed a sigh of relief when the results of the *Control Freak* quiz revealed you are not a Controller. But wait, not so fast! Believe it or not, there's another facet of Control, which is not constant, but rather at times can pop up when we least expect it. There is a potential, even in the best of us, given the right set of circumstances, to exhibit some characteristics of Control *freakiness*. It's called *Situational Control*.

I've heard, and even experienced both sides of this storyline which gets 'played out' with our GirlFriends. I would be surprised, if at some point you have not been touched by a similar chain of events. Ready? Ok, now promise you won't get *mad* at me. Just hear me out. I will give you an idea of what this *Game* might look like. I will call this *I Thought You Were My Friend Game*. Oh My!

You decide to start your own business. (No groaning, please) You have thought about it for a long time. You did your homework on the company and product, investigated the pluses and minuses, took the leap of faith, invested your money, and signed on the dotted line. You are now prepared and motivated to share your newfound venture. You are so excited that you even want to offer your GirlFriends the same 'opportunity' to join with you in this undertaking. How are we doing so far? Are you cringing yet?

Before we go any further, I am by *NO* means putting down any of these types of businesses. Just the opposite. I myself, have thoroughly enjoyed being involved with several similar companies, both as a customer, as well as a successful manager. They were some of the best times of my life in which I met several of my Forever Friends. I think they can be incredible opportunities, especially if your desire is to be in *Control* of your time, salary, and schedule. Now, those are good *Controls* to have!

Alright then, let me continue, please. ~

Your GirlFriend invites you to meet for coffee just to chat, she says. You get a babysitter, put on your cutest outfit, drive to the darling cafe, and now here comes your GirlFriend through the front door. You haven't seen her in awhile, so you're very excited to catch up on everything going on in her life, and sharing yours too.

She begins by giving you a big hug, then immediately hands you her pretty, brand spanking new, business card. It's called, *Let Me Step on You ~ Not your Mama's kind of Shoe Business!* I made it up. Isn't it cute? My husband didn't think so.

Anyway ~

Your GirlFriend then spends the next 2 hours telling you of her step by step plans and goals in her endeavor to be successful. She asks you nothing about how you're doing or your life. Before leaving, she gives you another hug and says with enthusiasm: "*I hope you will 'support' me in this.*" You tell her you are very happy and excited for her, and you really are.

Now you, the *Receiver*, goes home and immediately receives a text from your *Entrepreneurial* GirlFriend. She asks if you would be willing to have a party with your friends to help her get started. Again, she adds how much fun it would be working together, IF you joined her in this pursuit.

Have you ever struggled being on either side of a similar scenario, as described? Does it immediately conjure up any awkward or negative feelings? *IF* not, then you can bypass this next section completely. On second thought, you might know someone who may need to learn how to best deal with this type of situation. So, please continue reading. Did I just sound Controlling to you? I'm sorry. Do whatever you want!

Now, let's deal with the possible backlash that may ensue. If you genuinely feel you would like to accept any of the invitations your GirlFriend has given you, that's fantastic! God bless you. Go for it. End of story!

But, what *IF* after thinking it over, you decide you really don't feel comfortable or want to go forward with either invitation. What happens next? This is where things can get pretty *testy.* You are feeling:

a. *The product is too expensive for your budget.*

b. *You have little or no interest in the product.*

c. *You have little or no interest in the business for yourself.*

d. *You simply don't have time.*

e. *You don't want to put pressure on your GirlFriends to purchase anything.*

So, What's a Girl to DO?

Receiver GirlFriend has some choices to make in response to her *Entrepreneurial* GirlFriend's request. Let's pretend you are the *Receiver.*

1. You need to be open and honest about how you're feeling about this situation. Let her know you are happy for her, and appreciate the offers made.

2. Say *"No"* cheerfully, and without guilt. This may take some practice, especially *IF* you have 'people pleasing' tendencies. Ask the Lord for courage to speak the truth, in love.

3. Share how you value her friendship, and hope she will not be mad at you, or that your response will not cause any uneasiness in your relationship. The longer you allow the situation to go unaddressed, the more negatively it will impact you both. Remember, the *Elephant!*

4. Be sure to speak uplifting words to your GirlFriend and ask her to give you some other suggestions of ways you could be of encouragement to her.

Entrepreneurial Girlfriend needs to handle the *"No"* in a godly manner.

1. Allow yourself to be disappointed, however not at the expense of heaping anger, or by 'guiltifying' your GirlFriend.

2. Stay away from statements like: "*I thought you were my friend and would support me.*" Or, "*I would have done it for you.*"

3. Just because you would have said *"Yes"* to a Friend, don't give her the message "You should be like me." She's not, and that's ok.

4. The true test of a friendship is letting go of your unmet expectations and accepting your GirlFriend for who *she* is. Give her the freedom to say "No."

How do *you* react if your desires get *blocked* like this? We may not realize it, but we all put expectations or pressure to perform on others. I heard this saying: "*As long as everything goes exactly the way I want it, I can be totally flexible.*" If that explains you, I get it. It's ok to feel disappointed, if you were not thrilled with your GirlFriend's response. Just because you were initially unhappy or mad at her answer, doesn't mean you are a *Control Freak*. It simply means you are normal. Give yourself time to grieve.

Situational Control means from time to time, when push comes to shove, you will still be tempted to cross the line and start imposing your expectations on your GirlFriends! I can't express too strongly how this subtle *Control Game* can totally devastate a friendship. This is also true for *ALL* relationships, husband, children, siblings, coworkers, etc.

IF you are on the receiving end of a great *'puppet master'*, it's time to gently communicate to your GirlFriend you no longer are looking to *'dance on her strings'*. Express it in a kind way, naturally. You can't change the situation by Controlling a Controller, you can only change yourself, and tell her how you feel. This would be a great opportunity for each of you to express your expectations to one another. Remember, the higher your expectation, the greater your disappointments can be.

You can take charge of the relationship, in a positive way, by setting healthy boundaries. If she refuses to change her behavior, then you will need to consider the options of continuing to *do the dance*, cutting the *conductor's* strings, or perhaps walking away from the friendship for a time. We don't typically choose the circumstances which make us feel out of Control, but we do *always* choose the way we respond to them.

Hopefully, the one truth you will take away from this chapter is whenever you experience a *blocked desire* you have no Control over, you can immediately release it to God in prayer. Ask Him to help you respond in the Spirit and not in flesh. This last story comes from Luke 10:38-42. I sort of added my own little spin to it, which I think you may recognize.

Jesus was coming to dinner at the home of Mary and Martha. Can you imagine what that must have been like! What would you do to try to *impress* Him if He showed up at your door? Martha was a type A personality (a bit intense). She was making lots of preparations, possibly at the expense of other people's feelings. She had her own set of rules and expectations for everyone, especially her sister, Mary.

However, Mary was a type B personality (more laid back), who rarely gets overly excited about anything. Martha was having a difficult time trying *to get* Mary to follow her orders, for *order* in the house. She couldn't understand why Mary was not as concerned as she was about getting all these things done.

So, Mary decided to take Control of the situation herself and began running around the house like a 'chicken with her head cut off'! She was preparing the perfect Keto *pressure* cooker meal, setting the table with gorgeous new dinnerware from HomeGoods, and chargers and napkin rings courtesy of Pottery Barn.

She scurried around lighting all the Yankee candles, and of course, putting the finishing touches on the darling coffee filter wreath she was making for the front door. Have you seen those? Cute and easy, too! You never get a second chance to make a good first impression, you know.

Anyway ~

She was doing it all, while Mary just sat quietly at Jesus' feet, listening to Him speak. What was her problem anyway? Didn't she see all the work her sister was doing? How selfish and irresponsible could she be, thought Martha. So, after trying to *put the pressure on Mary* to do things her way, which wasn't working, she pulled out all the stops.

She took Jesus aside and tried to Control and 'womanipulate' Him too by saying, *"Don't you care that Mary isn't helping me?"* She tried to *get* Him to tell Mary to be like her and do what she was doing. Sometimes when a Controller can't Control you, they will try to Control what others think about you!

Jesus was having none of it, though, and went on to rebuke Martha in so many words. He said, *"Martha, Martha, you are so worried and upset over so many things. Just let Mary be Mary, she has chosen the better thing to do, and I won't take that away from her."* How embarrassing!

So, pretty much, Jesus was conveying to Martha to stop trying to Control everyone and everything around her. There's no need to 'guiltify' others to get them to do what you want them to do, or make them feel they need to be like you, Martha. Instead, let's sit back, relax and enjoy one another, and our time together, without all the drama. Life is too short!

I hope you enjoyed my modern day interpretation of this story!

So, What's a Girl to DO?

I encourage you to ask yourself the tough questions as it relates to areas you might be trying to Control in your GirlFriends. Stop using the *"That's just the way I am"* defense for not changing your ways. It sure isn't always the easiest thing for a *Control Freak* to do, but ask God or perhaps even a life coach to help you get Control of your Controlling habits.

* Let Jesus take the 'Wheel of your Life' by turning over Control to Him.

* Reconsider your expectations of your GirlFriends.

* Give up the right to always be right!

* Listen to what your GirlFriends think or feel concerning a situation.

* Allow your GirlFriend the freedom to be who she is. She is not you, and that's OK.

* Find a balance between holding on to and letting go of your 'womanipulating' ways.

Even if you admit to being a *Control Freak*, it isn't something you need to be stuck with forever. They say the first step to change is being mindful of your behavior, and the second step is taking responsibility by doing something about it.

I used to be a bit of a *Control Freak* in the past, however, I'm finally learning how to Control it! I think you *should* do the same! Oooops!

PART III

*** *Game Changers* ***

Forgiving a

GirlFriend is the

Gift

You Give Yourself ...

and Her!

CHAPTER 9
Sorry About That!

"Be kind and tenderhearted, forgive one another, AS God has forgiven you."

Ephesians 4:32

So, you find a piece of plastic in your expensive lobster dinner, and the server responds by saying, *"Sorry about that!"* Someone hits your vehicle with their shopping cart, then says in a flippant manner, *"Sorry about that!"* How many times have we heard that phrase? Now, I don't know about you, but for some reason, it drives me Cra-Cra!

It's usually a short and insensitive response to a not so pleasant situation. Do you think those are 'good enough' apologies? Perhaps in the grand scheme of things, they are. However, in my opinion, (and I have many) a quick or glib apology can sometimes be worse than saying nothing at all.

In these given scenarios, probably a day, a week, or a month will pass by, and they will be a distant memory, barely making it to the back of our minds. These are relatively easy circumstances to forgive and forget; however, what happens when a GirlFriend does or says something which deeply hurts you? Would a *"Sorry about that"* retort, or a no apology at all response be ok with you, then?

I'm sure we can all reflect on a time or two when we felt a deep sense of being wronged by someone: when a GirlFriend spread untruths about you, shared your personal story with another person, or maybe took a leadership role, she knew you really wanted. Maybe a parent disowned you, your husband cheated on you, or your child disappointed you and continues to do so. You fill in the blanks. Is it really necessary, or honestly, even possible for us to Forgive some misdeeds? Hmmm.

Results of a survey I read recently reported 73% of Americans to say there is someone in their life they simply cannot Forgive. That's a huge number of people walking around with a burden they were never meant to carry. Additionally, another 60 percent believe that Forgiving someone would depend on the offender apologizing or making changes FIRST! In order for you to Forgive a GirlFriend, do you believe she needs to apologize to you beforehand?

I'm thinking there might be a few of you who still recall the one-liner made famous in the 1970 movie *Love Story*, starring Ali McGraw and Ryan O'Neal. I remember the movie all too well. My husband and I sat watching it on the big screen, one cold and snowy December evening. The end of the movie caused me to sob so hard the black, non-waterproof mascara I perfectly applied earlier, generously poured down my young face and formed puddles of black goo all over my beautiful, new, white faux fur jacket! Whew!

Now, I know why they call these movies tear-jerkers. I couldn't stop the tears from flowing, nor my body from jerking out of control! I'm not sure what caused me to be more upset, the movie's conclusion or that I had just ruined my gorgeous new jacket. It could have been the fact we had just left our 11-month-old with a babysitter for the first time, ever! I think it honestly was the combination of all those things, plus the insecure feelings I was experiencing, realizing I was about to go through the labor and delivery process all over AGAIN, in 3 short months! Can anyone spell Hormones?

Anyway ~

Ali made her famous death-bed declaration heard around the world of "*Love means, NEVER having to say you're sorry.*" Now, please don't be mad at me for the movie spoiler, but I assumed IF you haven't heard the ending by now (50 years later), I'd save you from the torment of watching it yourself! People everywhere were not only repeating those words but were beginning to believe and act on its message, as well, myself included!

Maybe it was okay then to not say you were sorry. I guess if we offended a GirlFriend, we could simply justify our actions by telling ourselves we either didn't mean to hurt her, explain she was being overly sensitive, or perhaps we thought somehow she deserved it! Now, what if the tables were turned, and you were the one who did the hurting. Wouldn't you want your GirlFriends to offer Forgiveness to you? You *do* know that it works both ways. Sometimes you need to Forgive others, and other times, you want others to Forgive you, right?

Sorry about that Ali, but despite your heartfelt, popular saying, the truth is, *real* love means *NEEDING* to say you're sorry. Not only is it possible that we Forgive others, but it's *vital* that we do! It's essential to the spiritual, emotional, mental, and physical well-being of both the Forgiver and the Forgiven.

Before we delve deeper into the specific facets of what Forgiveness is, let's look at what Forgiveness is *NOT*. You might be surprised at what you find!

Forgiveness is **NOT**:

1. **Forgetting** what happened. It will never be a part of Forgiving, nor could it be.

2. **Pretending** it still doesn't affect you. It doesn't suddenly disappear.

3. **Condoning** what she did. This is not excusing her behavior. It was not ok.

4. **Trusting** your GirlFriend again. It takes time to rebuild it.

5. **Feeling** sad, hurt or disappointed doesn't mean you didn't Forgive her.

6. **Changing** the past. It is what it is. No *should of, could of or would of.*

7. **Depending** on her to admit her part. It's not based on *her* actions.

8. **Repaying** evil for evil. No taking things into your own hands.

9. **Getting** your GirlFriend to change *before* you Forgive her. If you need her to change *first* for you to be ok, you are still a prisoner of unforgiveness.

10. **Reconciling** is not the same as Forgiving. You may not remain friends.

What is your definition of Forgiveness?

DEFINITION of FORGIVENESS:

Mr. Webster says: To give up resentment against an offender. To cancel indebtedness. Grant pardon for an offense. Even as we look at the meaning of the word *pardon*, he describes it as "*An act of officially saying that someone who was judged to be guilty of an offense, will be allowed to go free and will not be punished.*"

Now, that's a tough pill to swallow! I know doing things God's way is not always going to be easy, and it's definitely not popular either. However, please don't misunderstand what I'm saying. Forgiving someone doesn't mean you always let your GirlFriend 'off the hook' if she has done something wrong. For example: If she stole money from you, you still need to hold her responsible for paying it back.

The difference is when you truly Forgive someone, you don't hold a grudge against her, or harbor ill will towards her, whether she repays you or not. If you're a believer, you have the Holy Spirit living in you, and He will guide you to choose the right response for each situation.

There have been thousands of books written, and sermons preached on the subject of Forgiveness. It's been addressed in the bible as many as 150 times, depending on which version you're reading. One thing I can say for sure is, Forgiveness is always a part of God's amazing *Game* plan for our lives. It's what the Christian faith is built on: God's love and Forgiveness to us.

Having spoken with thousands of women over the years, I've found far too many who are yet unclear about what Forgiveness really means, and how it gets worked out in their relationships. Now that we have a better understanding of its definition and some of the misconceptions surrounding it, let's begin to uncover a few of those components that make up Forgiveness.

Forgiveness is A DECISION

It is the decision you make to give up your right to hurt your GirlFriend because she hurt you first. God's Word has given us specific instructions concerning what to do when someone injures us. It's all summed up in this one word ~ *FORGIVE*! You might be asking yourself why should I Forgive a GirlFriend, even when I don't *feel* like it, or don't think she deserves it? Great question.

The Bible makes it apparent why in Matthew 6:14-15. "IF we Forgive others when they sin against us, *THEN* your heavenly Father will Forgive you. If you don't Forgive them, He won't Forgive you." As we can see, it's not a suggestion, it's a command. First, we must make the decision to Forgive our GirlFriend, so we ourselves can be Forgiven.

I know it's simple to say, but I recognize it's not an easy or natural thing for any of us to do. The world and everything inside us screams, '*No way; it's not fair!*' I know it doesn't appear to be, yet I think I can explain it like this. Remember what our parents used to tell us when we asked them why we needed to do something we didn't really want to do? Let's all say it together. "*Because I said so!*" Do you think they were saying that to be mean or wanted to punish you? I would say, in most cases, *NO*. They simply believed they knew what was best for us or were trying to protect us from potential harm.

How much more our heavenly Father loves us and knows what is in our best interest. He knows that harboring unforgiveness is destructive to us, and to our GirlFriends on the receiving end. Grace, being unmerited favor, means we *choose* to Forgive our GirlFriends as an act of our will and obedience to Him, not because they deserve it.

Our *Focus Verse also* tells us we must Forgive others in the *same way* Jesus has Forgiven us. Jesus is our example as He was betrayed by a friend, lied about, deserted by many, forsaken by the Father, stripped, tortured, hung on a cross, and died a horrific death for us. He had every right to be angry and not Forgive, yet He said, "Father, Forgive them, for they don't know what they are doing. Not My will, but Yours be done." Luke 23:34

Which brings us to the next reason we Forgive. It's because we ourselves have been abundantly Forgiven! 1 John 1:9 assures us, "IF we confess our sins, He is faithful and just to Forgive our sins, and to cleanse us from ALL unrighteousness." That means totally and completely, past, present, and future. So, which offenses then do we need to Forgive our GirlFriends for? *ALL* of them!

God's Word also claims He not only Forgives *ALL* our sins, but He blots them out and remembers them no more. Isaiah 43:25 tells us even *if* we try to remind Him of our misdeeds (which we sometimes do), He CAN'T recall them.

I am definitely not saying when a GirlFriend hurts us, we will never think of it again. That would be impossible because we are not God. Rather, Forgiveness is the ability to remember the offense without being angry or wanting to retaliate. We instead get to *choose* to think about our GirlFriend, and the hurtful circumstance, in the light of what God has done for *us*. We must then offer that same grace and Forgiveness to her. I love the quote from Corrie ten Boom, which says that "*Forgiveness is an act of the will, and the will can function regardless of the temperature of the heart.*" Now, that's tweetable, Corrie!

Forgiveness is A PROCESS

Making the decision to Forgive doesn't mean it's already accomplished. No, it's only the first step in a sometimes long process. It begins with an attitude of the heart that says, 'I am willing to be willing, God'. It takes time and work and is seldom, if ever, a one-time event. I wish I could tell you there's a shortcut or we could simply put in a rush order from Amazon Prime to hurry this process along.

I know for myself how much I hate constantly thinking about a painful situation so much, that my response is often to proclaim as Scarlett O'Hara did in the movie *Gone with the Wind.* "I'll think about it tomorrow!" The problem is, IF we don't work *through* the hurts and offenses the correct way, that's exactly what we *WILL* do. We'll think about it tomorrow, and the next day, and the day after that, too!

Simply put, it's like being sick and going to the doctors. Although, that's not always an easy feat either, as you will see. You must take the first steps by showing up at the doctor's office, signing in, then sitting in the waiting room, trusting help is on its way. After your name is called, you take your next steps down the long 'hall of shame' towards the dreaded scale. Immediately after being weighed in, they take your blood pressure. Of course, by now, it's registering off the charts due to the fact it's pretty much the same as it was the day you delivered your last child!

Next, you are led to the always freezing exam room, where you are instructed to disrobe and put on the lovely gown with the ties in the back. I will say no more. You are actually feeling worse now than when you arrived because of your *focus.* You're then required to sit on the cold, hard metal table with the rough, white, crinkly paper, and wait still longer for the doctor to come in. Next, the nurse enters, asks a few more questions, takes your temperature and listens to your racing heart, still a by-product of the scale's reading. You 'hang out' still more ~ in the room, of course!

The doctor finally arrives for 5 minutes, diagnoses the problem, and writes a prescription for you. Despite the fact that you did all the right things, you're not yet *feeling* any better than you did when you walked through the front door. Now, you go to the pharmacy, where you wait. You arrive home and finally get to ingest the first dose of the medicine which promises your healing. It still typically takes anywhere from a few hours to perhaps several weeks to experience any positive relief.

I sure hope you get the idea here!

What I am trying to say is, there is a process we all need to go through, whether going to a doctor or Forgiving a GirlFriend. Healing, either physical or emotional, doesn't happen overnight. It takes time to *feel* better even after *doing* all the right things. We take the first step when we open the door of our hearts by being willing. Then, we continue to follow the Great Physician's 'prescription' by applying Forgiveness as the recommended 'antibiotic'.

Needless to say, we will probably not immediately *feel* all warm and fuzzy towards our GirlFriend or ever forget what happened. Feelings are always followers~eventually. The opposite is also true. If we respond to our GirlFriend's hurts by choosing not to Forgive, those negative feelings will become toxic, *infecting* our body, mind, and spirit.

Forgiveness is FREEDOM

Forgiving a Girlfriend is allowing God the freedom to come into those wounded places in our lives and heal them. As we begin to release the bitterness and resentment and open our heart to His love and Forgiveness, He will meet us where we are. Instead many of us will hold tight to unforgiveness because we somehow believe we are punishing the offender.

But, it's really *us* who become sick and weak, slowly dying to all good things God has planned for us. We say when I *feel* right about it, or when she apologizes, or whatever you say to yourself to justify holding back your Forgiveness, *THEN*, I will *do* what is right. But, now is the time to Forgive, because we are commanded to, so God can Forgive us, and because we ourselves have been abundantly Forgiven.

I am sure many of you have had some pretty unforgivable things happen in your life, and I am not trying to make light of that. You might even say I don't understand what you've been through. You are absolutely right, I don't know your pain, but Jesus does. I also know staying stuck in the hurts of the past clouds everything in your lives right now, blocks you from hearing the voice of God, and keeps you from fully enjoying the present.

Even though there is nothing we can do to change the past, we *can* make a decision to accept it for what it was, learn and grow from it, and be willing to leave it where it belongs, as I did with 'Gail'. Philippians 3:13-14 encourages us to "Forget those things which are behind, I press forward to the higher upward call of Jesus."

We need to stop struggling to get something back from our GirlFriend in order for us to move forward. When we choose to pardon her, we are basically giving her freedom by saying, 'I will not bring up this situation again, or use it against you.' The bonus is, that in the process of Forgiving her, *YOU* are the one who will be set free! "Who Jesus has set free, 'she' is FREE indeed!" John 8:36

So, *IF* Forgiving is so important to God, and is necessary for our own well-being, why is it so many of us choose not to do it? Several reasons we remain consumed by unforgiveness is because we believe:

* The offense was too great.

* They didn't accept responsibility.

* They aren't truly sorry.

* They didn't ask for Forgiveness.

* They did it too many times.

* They did it deliberately.

* They need to be punished.

* You would feel like a hypocrite.

* You think you need to be friends with them.

What would you say is keeping you from Forgiving a GirlFriend, or anyone else today?

What is your typical response when confronted with a situation that needs Forgiveness? Do you sometimes feel justified in holding back your mercy and grace on your GirlFriend because of what she did? In Chapter 4, we discussed two of the negative ways we can respond to the harm inflicted on us by a GirlFriend: We can either Externalize or Internalize. You may not be the personality type that lashes out or tries to get even; instead, you may use the quiet, internal approach.

Your method of dealing with unforgiveness might be then to try to: suppress your thoughts and feelings, drink another glass of wine, or perhaps pop a few more pills to dull the pain. For some of us, our drug of choice is the obsessive talking about it to others and reminding ourselves of all the *shoulds* or *should nots* that occurred.

I know it *seems* to alleviate the pain temporarily, but the problem is GirlFriends, as Proverbs 16:24-25 says, "There is a way that seems right to a 'woman', but the end leads to death." Oh, perhaps not physical death, but the death of your joy, your peace, your hopes for the future, and your relationships. As we seek to cover up those wounds with these *bandaids*, we need to be aware that there is an infection brewing underneath it all. Here's the situation.

You may think if you don't come to terms with how the injuries affected you, magically, all your thoughts and feelings will somehow go away on their own. As you have probably figured out by now, they don't! Just because we *feel* we have a good reason for holding onto an offense by reacting in these misdirected manners, it certainly doesn't make it right.

Now, I think it's time for another one of my up close and personal stories. My sister, Jeanne, says I am full of them. At least, that's what I think she said!

I'm reminded of the time my daughter, Joy, got a terrible case of the flu. Her husband was out of town, and she was too sick to pick up her prescription. Because it was late in the evening, she asked me to go to the pharmacy for her, then spend the night at her house. I don't like driving at night, but as we all know, no matter how old our *kids* are, it's what we mothers do. Therefore, I went.

Before leaving the store, I thought I should purchase some over the counter medicine to prevent me from getting sick. So, I quickly grabbed some Airborne, which I heard worked well for others. I then jumped in the car, preparing for the long ride there. I decided I should probably take it immediately so it could begin working in my system.

After I ripped open the box, I noticed they pretty much looked like a chewable Vitamin C. So, instead of wasting any more time fumbling for my glasses and reading the instructions, I opened the bottle and popped two tablets in my mouth. I figured, IF one was good, two must be better, right?

I cannot do justice to the unbelievable scene which took place immediately following, but I will try. If you have ever taken Airborne, then you have already figured it out! Now, remember, it's late, I'm tired, my daughter is sick and needs me, I don't see very well at night, I don't want to get sick!

Within seconds after I began chewing, the tablets started *fizzing* inside my mouth! I started coughing, choking, and spitting them out all over the interior of my freshly cleaned car. They were everywhere: on the dashboard, the seats, the windows, the steering wheel, in my hair, and on my clothes. I had my bottle of water with me, so I decided to take a huge gulp to wash it all down. Not a good idea. They exploded even more in my throat now. By this time, I was literally *foaming in the mouth*.

Oh, did I mention I was sitting right in the middle of a dark, almost empty Walmart parking lot? I was scared to get out of the car, but I had to finish getting the remainder of it out of my mouth quickly! Listen, IF there were *bad guys* anywhere near me that evening, trust me when I say, they would have been more afraid of me than I was of them!

After I got back in the car, I turned on the lights and put on my glasses to see how this had all gone so terribly wrong. I decided to read the directions *AFTER* I took them. It read: *"Drop ONE tablet into an 8 oz glass of water. WAIT for it to stop fizzing, then drink."* Too late! The damage had already been done.

Just then, my now concerned daughter called to ask what was taking me so long. I said, "You wouldn't believe me If I told you." Despite her being really sick, we had a good laugh after I finally arrived there, safe and sound. Guess what? I never did get sick! Thank you, God. Why do I tell you this story? I was beginning to wonder about that myself!

Stay with me now ~

It's like we can think in our own mind, what we are doing is right, like staying mad at someone. We might even feel justified because we know others who would have done the same thing. But, IF we don't follow the 'instructions' *exactly* the way they were intended by the 'Maker', not only will we *not* get the desired results, but we will be left with a great big mess to clean up after! That's what not Forgiving a GirlFriend looks like!

We need to know what God's Manual says, and learn *how* to apply His truths to our situations in the correct way, or it will cause much heartache and pain. It's not only you that gets *infected*, but everyone, or as in my case, everything else around you can get pretty 'messed up' too. Hebrews 12:15 warns us to "Watch out that no poisonous root of bitterness grows up among you to trouble you, and corrupts many." Real freedom begins when we, by faith, choose to become *Better* and not *Bitter*!

Here are some consequences you will experience IF you choose not to Forgive:

*Angry *Resentful *Bitter *Vengeful *Judgmental *Lonely

*Depressed *Untrusting *Self-Absorbed *Cynical *Joyless

*Sick   *Hopeless   *STUCK*

Do any of these *side effects* have a hold on you? Circle which ones.

So, What's a Girl to DO?

Here are some action steps I found helpful in getting from the negative, all-consuming thoughts and feelings, to Forgiveness.

1. *Pray, ask God to help you Forgive your GirlFriend the same way He Forgives you.*
2. *See her the way Jesus does, flaws and all, yet loved and precious.*
3. *Return a blessing rather than a curse or insult. Pray for God's best for her.*
4. *Put off thinking, talking, and reliving the negative thoughts.*
5. *Look for how God can use your experience to teach and strengthen you.*

Remember, God will not waste anything you go through in your life. Romans 8:28 says, "All things work together for good, to those who love the Lord." It doesn't say all things are good or God causes bad things to happen. It means no trial, no hurt, no no, nothing, will come into our lives that God can't use for good *IF* we trust in Him. "As for you, what you intended for harm, God meant it for good." Genesis 50:20

Can you think of a situation which in itself was negative, but God turned it into something positive? What valuable lesson did you take away from it?

_____

_____

Maybe *YOU* are the one who hurt a GirlFriend? Perhaps deeply. You made some mistakes and didn't handle a situation in the best way. There are times, even though you've humbled yourself before God, and your GirlFriend has Forgiven you, but you still have difficulty Forgiving yourself.

Another Quick Story ~

I was in a hurry yesterday, late for an appointment. As I was quickly backing out of our garage, I heard a loud *BANG!* I smashed right into my husband's new car and did damage to *BOTH* of our vehicles. Even though mine is 13 years old, I love it and have always taken meticulous care of it. It didn't even have one scratch on it ~ well, it does *NOW*!

I will not share everything which transpired after that, but all I can say is I apologized profusely to my husband for my carelessness several times. I called myself some pretty unflattering names, and even vowed to turn my driver's license and car keys over to the State! Obviously, I was traumatized! Even though he quickly Forgave me (it took about an hour for the shock to wear off), I still felt horrible. Had I continued apologizing over and over, he probably would have become very irritated with me as it would have meant I didn't believe he Forgave me the first time he said he did. I was actually harder on myself than he was.

That's often the way we act with God. Think how He must feel when we keep reminding Him of our same sins over and over, which He has already Forgiven us for! Let me ask you this question. How many of your sins were still in the future when Jesus died for you on the cross? That's correct, *ALL* of them!

So, how can we say we believe God enough to accept *HIS* Forgiveness, yet turn around and not Forgive ourselves? Obviously, If we don't Forgive ourselves, it means we don't believe in His promise to us. When we make mistakes or *fall down*, God doesn't get *mad* at us, nor does He turn His back on us. Instead He runs towards us to pick us up! Let yourself off the hook, GirlFriends because HE does! We will cover this further in our final chapter.

One Last example ~ I promise !

Several years ago, I taught a women's group at our church called Between Friends. One evening one of the ladies made a comment that I was shocked to hear her say. Or should I say, what I *thought* I heard her say. She noticed my obvious look of surprise, so I asked her to repeat it. She did. It was not at all what I had initially thought she said. I didn't think much of it; however, my sweet GirlFriend did. She kept attending the class, but I observed during the weeks following, she had become quieter than her usual bubbly self. One evening, after everyone left, I felt compelled to go find her.

I literally ran up to her in the parking lot and asked her if we could speak. You know what I asked her. "*Are you Mad at Me?*" She was very quick to say "*YES*"! Here I am, the leader, and what had I done? Bequi was originally from Lima, Peru, and spoke with an accent. She shared how she had always struggled with speaking the

English language fluently and had been embarrassed on occasion when she had been misunderstood. Oh great!

Now, in what I like to call my BC days, Before Christ, I would have *dismissed* her comment and assured her she speaks perfectly. Perhaps I would have said she shouldn't feel that way, or that embarrassing her was not my intention, or anything in order to not take responsibility for the fact that my comment hurt her. So, I thanked her for her honesty, and said I was sorry for my careless words. I went on to assure her I'd be more sensitive to her in that area.

Finally, I asked IF she would be willing to Forgive me. She immediately did, and also thanked me for seeking her out. God restored our relationship and knitted our hearts together even more than before. Why? First of all, because she was willing to be honest and Forgiving. Next because I chose to humble myself, listen to her heart, sincerely apologize for my words, and ask for her Forgiveness.

I recognize that not all relationships can be mended and brought back to the same state they were in prior to an offense, despite doing all the right things. It doesn't mean you didn't Forgive your GirlFriend. There are simply times when one or both of you are unwilling to admit their part and work through the issue at hand.

It could also be that the damage done with words or actions have passed the point of no return. Fortunately for us, Bequi accepted my apology. A couple years after that conversation, she went 'home' to be with the Lord. I miss her and am blessed to have called her my Friend!

Here are the very best guidelines I have found helpful in restoring broken relationships. They are taken from the book *The 5 Languages of Apology* by Gary Chapman.

1. *Express Regret ... I am sorry*

2. *Accept Responsibility ... I was wrong*

3. *Make Restitution ... What can I Do to make it right?*

4. *Genuine Repentance ... I will try not to do that again.*

5. *Request Forgiveness ... Would you be willing to Forgive me?*

There is power in a sincere apology. Understanding and applying these 5 principles can greatly enhance all your relationships. It doesn't always mean your GirlFriends will accept it. As I have already shared with you, there have been times in my life I believe I responded to difficult circumstances God's way, yet a friend refused to restore the relationship. I'm sad to say those friendships ended!

I'm not sure why, but today it seems easier for people to just 'unfriend' a GirlFriend they once held dear, instead of making every effort to resolve the conflict.

So, What's a Girl to DO?

Who are you still holding accountable for what they did to you?

Choose ONE hurt (at a time) you need to Forgive her for.

Release it totally to God, by an act of your will.

What specific steps can you take to move towards applying God's love and Forgiveness in this situation?

_____

_____

REMEMBER......Forgiveness is a **Decision**, it's a **Process,** and finally, it's **Freedom ~** as we allow God to transform our hearts and minds! Forgiving a GirlFriend might never change her, but I can say with certainty, it *will* definitely change you!

All You Need is Love!

However, a Little

Chocolate

Every Now and Then

Never Hurts!

CHAPTER 10
Are You Mad at Me too, God?

"God showed His love by sending Christ to die for us, while we were yet sinners."

Romans 5:8

Well, I guess you could say, we saved the best topic for the final quarter, the bottom of the tenth inning, or ok, the last chapter. In Part I of *Girls Rule,* we Discovered the importance of having GirlFriends, along with Exploring the different types of GirlFriends.

We learned in Part II in *The Rule Breakers* section, God's ways of doing life together in relation to the *Games* GirlFriends *play* such as: Gossip, Offenses, Avoidance, Jealousy, Rejection, and Control. We sure are complex creatures, aren't we? I just love the saying attributed to Joyce Meyer, which states: *"I may not be where I want to be, but thank God, I'm not where I used to be"*! No one, not you or me is perfect, but we keep striving to become more like Jesus every day, as we trust Him to "complete the great work He began in us." Philippians. 1:6

Finally, in *The Real Game Changers* portion in Part III, we Uncovered the many complex dynamics of Forgiveness. Now, we'll conclude our book with *Are You Mad at Me Too, God,* where we will Examine the topics of Loving God, Loving Others, and Loving Ourselves.

Let me begin with this amazing statement: "Not only is God *NOT* mad at you, but He is *madly* in *LOVE* with you!" Can we even begin to comprehend or take in this great truth?

GOD'S LOVE

Now, being the spiritual woman I obviously am, let me ask you the same question Tina Turner asked in her famous song title. So, "*What's Love Got to Do with It?*" As far as God is concerned, I believe the answer to that question is simply ~ *EVERYTHING!* We've already established everyone wants to be Loved and accepted, right? I can assure you that you are wholly and completely Loved and cherished by the One who created the entire universe, and everyone and everything in it.

We can't receive any more of God's Love than we already have right at this moment. It doesn't happen by trying to be good enough, praying harder, attending church more often, or whatever we think needs to be done to *win* God's approval. In our *Focus Verse*, we read God Loved us so much, He was willing to give up His only Son for us. He didn't do that *AFTER* we got all *cleaned up* or *worked on* ourselves, but rather *BEFORE* we did any of those things; "While we were yet sinners, Christ died for us." Now, that's what Love has to do with it!

Knowing how much He Loves us, is slow to anger, and doesn't hold our sins against us, has totally changed not only what I think about Him in my *head*, but it has also completely transformed my *heart* toward Him. He is the exact opposite of Who I believed He was, when I was younger.

I imagined Him sitting on His golden throne in heaven, just watching and waiting for me to do something wrong, so He could punish me. Pretty sad, I know! I also believed IF I died before confessing all those wrongs to Him, I would go straight to hell. Do not pass *'GO'*, and do not collect anything!

Thinking God might find something to be mad at me about, terrified me so much, that whenever I confessed my sins to the priest every Saturday, I would always say the words 'innumerable times'. I used them to describe how often I 'might' have disobeyed my parents! I wanted to be sure to cover *all my bases* in the event I missed a sin or two.

On occasion, I could actually hear the priest chuckle behind the dark, mesh screened wall, which separated us. Of course, my contrite admissions certainly didn't move him to show any mercy on my poor, little, sorry soul. Usually, he still had me pray the entire rosary as my penance. Perhaps hearing my mantra each week led him to believe I wasn't truly contrite!

I had always *hoped* God might be a little easier on me than the priests were, though. I *hoped* He would use some sort of sliding scale, or grade me on a curve, when He judged me. I *hoped* all the good things I did would somehow outweigh the bad things I thought, said, or did!

Now that I know God in a real and personal way now, I am so elated to inform you there is *NO* need for me or you to fear Him as I did. He extends to each of us "A perfect Love which casts out all fear. If we are afraid, it is for fear of punishment, and this shows that we have not fully experienced His perfect Love."1 John 4:18.

He never, ever plays the *Now, I Gotcha Game* with His children, as we sometimes freely do with our GirlFriends. Now we have a *real hope*. Oh, it's not the 'I sure hope so' kind, as I just described. Instead, it's a *hope* and trust in His Love and promises for us. Rather than being a mean, judgmental God, who is waiting to *get us*, He is a kind, gentle and Loving Father,

Who is on our side, and is our greatest cheerleader. "There is nothing, no *NOTHING*, that can ever separate us from His Love." Romans 8:31

How we think about God does matter, and what we believe He thinks about us matters even more. In the event your relationship with your earthly father or father figure was less than perfect, this truth that God loves you unconditionally might be a foreign concept to you. Perhaps your father was abusive, distant or absent. If so, that relationship could taint your view of a heavenly Father.

You might either want to run from God, be angry at Him, or simply be indifferent and want nothing to do with Him. It may be your misguided religious background or a lack of knowledge concerning Him, that distorts your perception of who He truly is. Because of these life experiences, it's possible it could take more time for you to believe and connect to a Loving and caring God.

As with our GirlFriends, the more time we spend getting to know them, the more we can have trust and confidence in their character. As we are consistently encouraged by God's Love letters to us in His Word, godly teachers, and fellowship with other Christ followers, we will begin to understand and eventually experience God's Love for us.

What about you: are you perhaps still thinking God is mad or disappointed in you too? Can you honestly admit you might even have been *mad* at Him now? It's ok to answer "*YES.*" It's not the unpardonable sin. Tell Him how you feel, as He's always there ready to listen. I believe He can handle us being upset with Him, for a season. Just don't stay stuck there too long. Remember, He is the one Who created you, so

He already knows *EVERYTHING* about you, and Loves you anyway.

I must *confess*, there have been times in my own life when I've been disappointed, let down, and even *mad* at God too! I expected He would answer my prayers in a certain way and when He didn't, it caused me much self-induced heartache. When life didn't make sense, and I couldn't come up with any good enough reasons why He said *"No,"* I would struggle dealing with all the unanswered questions.

Even now I don't always understand why certain situations happen, but I ultimately make the decision to surrender to His sovereignty, and put my trust in Him alone, knowing He is trustworthy. After all, isn't that what our faith is all about anyway ~ believing even when we cannot see?

Speaking of *seeing,* my beautiful GirlFriend, Tierney, sent me a lovely wooden sign this week which reads: *"God is NOT Mad at You!"* Don't you just love it? Sometimes we just need a literal *sign* to remind us of God's unconditional love for us. Hey, whatever it takes!

Changing our negative thought patterns, and replacing our misconceptions with God's Truth takes time and practical application until these habits become a way of life for us! IF we don't believe God loves us and has our best interest at heart, we could stay *mad* at Him for a very long time, or in some cases, forever. If we continue to discount His Word, and focus on ourselves and our own pain, we will never be able to move forward in our lives in freedom and peace. I don't mean to be disrespectful here ~ but, here comes the *but.*

We must be careful not to treat God as if He is our very own personal *Santa Claus.* We make our list, and check it twice, and when we don't get exactly *what* we want *when* we want it, we stop believing in Him and His goodness. I know that sounds a bit harsh, but sometimes I think we *do* behave like that, don't we? I'm sure I'm not the only one who has ever felt that way. At least I hope not. Come on now Girlfriends, help me out here!

God *does* want us to make our desires and requests known to Him. And yes, He does always answer our prayers, as He says He will. Yet, sometimes the answer is a *"No."* It's ok to feel disappointed, and we need to take time to grieve. Other times, the answer is *"Wait."* Definitely not one of my greatest strengths. God's Word explains it well, when it says: "For my thoughts are not your thoughts, neither are your ways my ways, declares the Lord. For as the heavens are higher than the earth, so are my ways higher than your ways, and my thoughts than your thoughts." Isaiah 55:8-9.

Even though the circumstances we find ourselves in may not be good, faith is believing that God *IS* good, all the time, and that He Loves us no matter what is happening around us.

LOVING OTHERS

So, what kind of Love is this that He has poured out on us, and wants us to extend to others? It's the kind of Love which is laid out in 1Corinthians 13:4-8, often referred to as the 'Love Chapter'. In its original Greek, the word 'Love' used here is an *agape* Love, which translates into meaning a *divine* Love.

"Love is patient and kind. Love is not jealous, or boastful, or proud, or rude. It does not demand its own way. It is not irritable, and it keeps no record of being wronged. It does not

CHAPTER 10: ARE YOU MAD AT ME TOO, GOD?

rejoice about injustice, but rejoices whenever the truth wins out. Love never gives up, never loses faith, is always hopeful, and endures through every circumstance. Paul describes it as "a more excellent way."

Doesn't it seem impossible for us to have a Love like this for our GirlFriends? You're right, it *IS* impossible, in our own strength! You already know from your own interactions with them, this *agape* Love surpasses what we are equipped to give throughout the mad, sad and bad times we experience.

However, IF God has asked us to do something like "Love one another *AS* He has Loved us", it means He has already provided us with everything we need for it to be accomplished. Only as we surrender to Him, and allow Him to fill us with *HIS* Love can we experience Loving a GirlFriend who has hurt us in the same way He does.

The bible says, "The greatest measure of Love is when we lay down our lives for our friends." John 15:13. Uhh, I know what you're thinking. You didn't *sign up* for this one! Well, more than likely you will never be required to give up your physical life for another person. Instead, This "laying down of our lives" requires a practical working out in our everyday circumstance. As believers, we have all been the recipients of this Perfect Love when Jesus sacrificed Himself for us.

Now, His Love *compels* us to Love one another by putting the needs or desires of our GirlFriends on a level with our own. It's about being self~less rather than self~ish. Philippians 2:3-4 says: "Do nothing out of selfish ambition or empty pride, but in humility consider others more important than yourselves. Each of you should look out not only for your own interests but also for the interests of others."

It's not always about making the huge sacrifices for our GirlFriends either. It's the giving of ourselves in the everyday moments. We can 'lay down our lives' by praying for a friend, preparing a meal, apologizing first, sending a 'real' card, preferring her choice of activity, taking her kids for the day, or however the Lord leads you.

So, What's a Girl to DO?

---

1. What specific ways can you "lay down your life" for a GirlFriend this week?

---

2. Meditate on 1Corinthians Chapter 13. Write the areas of Love which need improving in your life. Choose one to be intentional about changing this week.

LOVING YOURSELF

Several times in the bible we are instructed to follow Jesus' greatest commandment to: "Love the Lord your God with all our heart, soul, and mind and strength, and your neighbor AS yourself." Luke 10:27. We just covered the first two commands in the verse of Loving God, and Loving Others. The ending of the verse states we are to love our neighbors, 'as ourselves,' which means *in the same way*!

Many of us have either overlooked or ignored those last two words. Just as important as how we think about God, it's also significant what we think about ourselves. It could be one of the reasons we have difficulty getting along with our GirlFriends. We don't truly Love, or even *like* ourselves! IF that's true of you, I would venture to say it will be very challenging, if not impossible, to Love others in the manner God asks us to.

I believe as women, many of us are overly concerned about our physical appearance, don't you agree? We critique ourselves carefully and usually find one or more things we dislike about ourselves, then tend to *focus* on those imperfections. But, if we can't Love and feel secure in who we are, how can as we possibly Love someone else.

Perhaps you are mad at yourself. Sometimes, we are our own worst enemy. We all sin, and fall short of what God expects, and even what we expect of ourselves. We don't always make the best decisions in life, as we discovered in our *Games* GirlFriends play section. Just as I have shared with you my own shortcomings, it's natural to feel bad, to have a 'guilty conscience', or even grieve the things we've done wrong, especially if it caused harm to a GirlFriend.

However, we must learn how to separate our identity, (who we really are) from our behavior (what we did). It's important to determine if the thoughts we have about ourselves are destructive *condemnations* or are healthy *convictions*, which are characterized as a "Godly sorrow which leads us to repentance (change)." 2 Corinthians 7:10. God wants us to Love ourselves, and have a positive self image. We are not to have a 'beating ourselves up' type of mentality. In order to make real life changes, instead we need to replace those thoughts with a 'building ourselves up' perspective.

Our self-acceptance is not only focusing on loving ourselves more, rather it's seeing ourselves in the light of who God says we are. He tells us throughout His Word how Remarkably and Wonderfully made we are, how Deeply we are Loved, how Completely we are Forgiven, and how Perfect we are in His sight. When we keep our eyes *fixed* on Jesus and His truths, we will realize how loved and valued we are, only then we will have the capacity to truly Love God, Others, and Ourselves!

So, What's a Girl to DO?
---

1. *Get to know the real God by spending quality and quantity time with Him in Prayer, Worship, Studying and Applying His Word, and Enjoying Christian fellowship.*

2. *Consciously weed out the lies we believe about God and ourselves, and replace them with truths of Who He is, and who He says we are.*

3. *Once we accept God's grace for ourselves, we are able to extend it to those around us.*

Well, we certainly have covered, and hopefully *uncovered* many of God's Truths in these 10 chapters. I pray the godly principles I've laid out on these pages will continue to be a source of encouragement, wisdom, and understanding as you *Play* this *Game* of *Life* together with your GirlFriends.

Pray without ceasing.

Get over offenses quickly.

Accept what you can't change.

Be happy for your GirlFriends.

Be patient with yourself and others.

Know God loves you unconditionally.

Refuse to waste time on negative thinking.

*Speak the truth, in love to your GirlFriends.

*Forgive yourself and your GirlFriends quickly.

*Believe God has a wonderful plan and purpose for you.

*Accept yourself, and your GirlFriends as God accepts you!

*Think and speak only kind words about yourself and others.

*Spend time with GirlFriends you love, and who love you back.

My Prayer for You:

*"I pray that Christ will be more and more at home in your hearts, living within you as you trust in Him. May your roots go down deep into the soil of God's marvelous Love, and may you be able to **feel** and **understand**, as all God's children should, how* long, *how wide, how deep, and how high His Love really is, and to experience this Love for yourselves. Though it is so great that you will never see the end of it, or fully know or understand it. And so, at last you will be filled up with God Himself." Ephesians 3:17-19*

FINAL WORDS:
So, What's a Girl to Do, Now?

Having spent this entire book talking about our GirlFriends, in a good way, of course, I would be remiss IF I didn't introduce you to My Forever Friend, and the Love of My Life. Please let me share with you a few reasons why I love Him so much.

He never criticizes me.

He understands me.

He gives the best gifts.

He is a great listener.

He never says, *"I told you so."*

He is available day and night.

He is always honest with me.

He picks me up when I am down.

He never makes me feel inferior.

He is understanding and compassionate.

He gives me the freedom to make mistakes.

He forgives me when I do something wrong.

He encourages me every minute of every day.

He is always there for me no matter where I am.

He knows what I am going to say, even before I say it.

He loves spending quality and quantity time with me.

He has been with me in the wonderful and horrible times.

He loves me unconditionally, always has, and always will!

Well, as you can see, I could go on and on about my Friend, but I think you may have already figured out Who He is. No one could be that *PERFECT*, except for Him, of course. He is the One who sticks closer than any brother.

His name is Jesus Christ!

Do you know Him? No, I don't mean do you know facts *about* Him. I am speaking about really *knowing* Him in a deep and intimate way. I'm sure many of you reading this already *do* love and have a personal relationship with Jesus. But, in the event you don't or are unsure, I want to give you the opportunity to have your entire life changed forever, beginning today.

What does He require from us to do this? *Everything.* Lay it all down: Your Plans for His, your Desires for His, your Thoughts for His, your Ways for His. Believe He has a better plan for your life than you do. There's no need to strive to accomplish this. It's a *'Come As You Are'* invitation. No need to clean up your act, hide behind a mask, or try to be someone you're not. He takes you right where you are and begins to transform you into the person He created you to be, in His time and in His way.

We talked about "The greatest measure of love is when you lay down your life for your friend." Well, that's exactly what He has already done for you and Me. He is now asking you to do the same for Him. He came into the world to give us abundant life here, and eternal life in heaven. Our part is to accept this *'Gift'* He has given us.

"For by Grace (unmerited favor) you have been saved, through Faith, it's not of yourself (not being good enough). It is the Gift of God, NOT of works, so no one may boast." Ephesians 2:8-9

So, what have you got to lose? Give your life to Jesus today. I promise you it will be the best decision you will ever make!

Now ~ for the final time ~ I will ask you this question:

So, What's a Girl to DO, Now?

It's very simple. I will give you a few facts to give you the assurance you made this decision today, once for all. More than the words you say, it's the attitude of your heart that brings you into the family of God. Are you ready?

1. God has a wonderful plan for your life.

"God so loved the world, He gave His one and only Son, that whoever believes in Him shall not perish, but have everlasting life." John 3:16

2. Man is sinful and separated from God. *"All have sinned and fall short of the Glory of God." Romans 3:23*

3. Jesus Christ is God's ONLY provision for our sin. Jesus said, *"I am the Way, the Truth, and the Life. No one comes to the Father, except through Me."John 14:16*

4. We must individually *receive* Jesus as Savior and Lord, then we can know and experience God's love and

plan for our life. *"As many as received Him, to them He gave the right to become children of God, even to those who believe in His name." John 1:12*

Receiving or accepting Jesus involves turning from yourself and your ways of doing things (repentance) to trusting Him to forgive you. It's not enough to only intellectually acknowledge Jesus as the Son of God, and that He died on the cross for you. Nor is it sufficient just to have an emotional experience. You receive Jesus by faith, and by an act of your will, not by your thoughts and feelings alone.

If this prayer below expresses the desire of your heart to accept Jesus, then I invite you to ask Him to come into your heart and life right now.

Say out Loud:

"Jesus, I am a sinner, and I need You. Thank you for dying on the cross to take away ALL my sins, past, present, and future. I open the door of my heart and receive You as my Lord and Savior. I surrender control of my life to You. Make me the person You want me to be. Thank you for forgiving me, and for giving me eternal life. Amen.

If you have said this prayer in sincere faith, Praise God! You are now a Christian. How can you know for sure? Because Jesus said it is true in 1 John 5:11

"God has given us eternal life, and this life is in His Son. He who has the Son has life. He who does not have the Son does not have life. These things I have written to you who believe, in order that you may KNOW you have eternal life.

You may want to write your name on this page, along with today's date, as a reminder of your commitment to Jesus, in faith.

Next Steps to Growth:

1. Attend church regularly. Find a Christ-centered church.

2. Read your Bible daily. Begin in the book of John.

3. Pray. Talk to God the same way you talk to a Friend.

4. Worship. Fill your mind and heart with Psalms and Christian music.

5. Fellowship. Spend time with Christian Friends.

Oh, and Welcome into the Family of God, Sister!

NAME:_____ DATE:_____

"I Thank My God

Every Time

I Remember You!"

Philippians 1:3

With Special Thanks:

Having an idea and turning it into a book is way more difficult than it seems, both emotionally and physically. It was immensely challenging yet rewarding, and could never have happened without the community of my loving and supportive family and GirlFriends who played an intricate part in getting it to the finish line.

To My Husband, Tony: What can I say to you? It would take another entire book to express to you my love and gratitude, but I don't have that much time left to write one! Thank you for your profound and unwavering belief in me and in the message of this book to GirlFriends everywhere. You graciously and patiently allowed me to process my own 'Games' each day, as you gently expressed your invaluable insights. You also saved us lots of money by being my very own personal counselor, and you know I needed and appreciate that. Thank you for always being my greatest cheerleader in Life. I'll Love You, Forever!

To My Children: Mike Tullio, Steve Tullio, Joy Joiner, and their spouses, Meadow Tullio, Sara Tullio, and John Joiner. See, I actually did finish the book! I always said "Good things come to those who wait, and wait..." I can not even begin to put into words the depth of my love and appreciation for each of you. I have been truly proud, honored, and blessed to be your Mother. You have been the best part of my life, and my reason for living! I'll Love you Always!

To my Grandchildren: Rachael, Brandon, Alex, Tyson, Joshua, Annie, and Chloe. Always remember, you are never too young or too old to make your dreams come true, with God's help, and lots of hard work. Thank you for giving me complete JOY every day of my life. I love you each sooooo much!

To My Sister, Jeanne: I am grateful that I have been doubly-blessed having you as my sister and my GirlFriend from birth. I appreciate your always saying to me: "You always have a story". For the first time ever, you were RIGHT! They came in handy for this book, and now, everyone else knows it's true too! You are the most generous, caring, and courageous person I know, and I do Love You MORE!

To Annette Burkholder: Your relentless love and support as a GirlFriend and in the writing of this book are immeasurable. Thank you for pushing me to finally complete it. Had it not been for you, it would have been buried in a trash pile in a landfill somewhere...literally. You have shown me what a Faithful Friend looks like, and for that I love you, and will be forever indebted to you!

To Valerie Ellery: Well, GirlFriend, we did it! Lots of blood, sweat, tears, and many hours and days being 'sequestered' at the Hilton unscrambling my brain! I am thankful for the teacher in you who took 'control', by helping me FOCUS and organize my thoughts enough to put on paper. I can honestly say, this book would never have been possible without you! I love You my true 'Warrior Woman', GirlFriend!

To Tierney Abel: Your encouragement and generosity cannot be underestimated. Thanks to you and David for opening your lovely home to me, and for being a respite, refuge, and refreshment during some difficult days during my writing and in life. Your soothing words and hospitality mean more to me than you could ever imagine!

To Dr. Sharon Otis: I am incredibly grateful for you, my 'sparkling', Sanguine GirlFriend. Your unconditional love and light shine bright like diamonds in my life. Thank you for always speaking your uplifting words of wisdom to me throughout the sometimes grueling process.

This book would not exist without this loyal community of exceptional GirlFriends and the ways each of you have touched my life in a significant way. I have received much inspiration, wisdom, encouragement, love, and prayers from all of you. Thank you for always allowing me to be myself!

In no particular order:

Susan Frey, Sue Brock, Debbie Kelly, Sandi Burke, Dr. Susan McSwain, Vickie Callahan, Rose Schenk, Rita Kalimon, Cindy Scott, Kim Dudas, my **GirlFriends from God** and **Between Friends** Groups!

If there is anyone I did not mention or if you feel I left you out, I am sorry. Please, do not be Mad at Me!

To You, Almighty God: I praise and bow down before You, for You alone are the only One worthy of all praise. Thank You for surrounding me with the most amazing family and GirlFriends imaginable. We both know without You, I wouldn't have either. Even though I may not have acted like it at times, I am honored and grateful that You enabled and equipped me to finish well, just as You promised. I sure do hope You like it!

Endnotes

Introduction:
Sticks and Stones Quote: *The Christian Recorder*, 1862.

Chapter 1:
It's Such a Girl Thing

Lewis, C.S. Quote: *"Friendships are Born..."*
https://www.overallmotivation.com/quotes/cs-lewis-quotes-friendship-heaven-love/
Symptoms of Depression.
https://www.webmd.com/depression/guide/detecting-depression#1
Maya Angelou Quote: *When You Know Better.*
https://www.goalcast.com/2017/04/03/maya-angelou-quotes-to-inspire-your-life/

Chapter 2:
The Blessings of GirlFriends

Let Me Go Lover: Jenny Lou Carson, Al Hill, Columbia Records, by Felix Jackson, 1954.
https://en.wikipedia.org/wiki/Let_Me_Go,_Lover!

Balcony People, Landorf, Joyce (Nashville: Thomas Nelson, 1984)
Boundaries, by Dr. Henry Cloud and Dr. John Townsend. October 3, 2017, HarperCollins, Zondervan.

Chapter 3:
Well Bless Her Heart!

Gossip in Your Workplace Probably Does More Good Than Harm.
(https://www.psychologytoday.com/blog/out-the-ooze/201504/gossip-in-your-workplace-probably-does-more-good-harm)
In HRZone, Siftmedia, U. K. F. T. (2015, June 10).

Gossip 3 Billion Dollar Industry.
https://theweek.com/articles/484520/3-billion-celebrity-gossip-industry-by-numbers
Meltzer, Bernard: *Is it Kind?*
https://www.brainyquote.com/quotes/bernard_meltzer_157511

Chapter 4:
She Makes Me So Mad!

Osteen, Joel: December 10, 2019
https://www.goodreads.com/quotes/8764559-every-day-we-have-plenty-of-opportunities-to-be-upset
Vanzant, Iyanla: How to turn a Hard conversation into a Carefrontation
https://www.pinterest.ch/pin/422282902546031263/

Chapter 5:
Where's the Elephant?

Powell, John: *Why Am I Afraid to Tell You Who I Am? Fontana, 1969*

Meyer, Joyce: Two Kinds of Pain
https://www.goodreads.com/quotes/404435-there-are-two-kinds-of-pain-the-pain-of-change

Chapter 6:
Eat Your Heart Out!

Didion, Joan: Vogue, Jun 1961 *Jealousy is dissatisfaction with oneself.*
http://quotegeek.com/literature/joan-didion/7143/

Chapter 7:
What About Me?

Lydgate, John, 15 Century Monk/Lincoln, Abraham, September 2, 1858, Clinton Illinois, Lincoln-Douglas Debate. '*Some of the People*" quote.

Nouwen, Henri J.M., Rejection quote.
https:/www.azquotes.com/author/10905-
Henri_Nouwen/tag/rejection

Surprising Facts about Rejection
https://www.psychologytoday.com/us/blog/the-squeaky-
wheel/201307/10-surprising-facts-about-rejection
Perceived Rejection
https://psychcentral.com/lib/good-news-if-you-often-feel-
rejected/

Chapter 8:
You Don't Own Me!

Gore, Leslie: *You Don't Own Me.* Mercury Records, Written by
John Madera, David White, 1964
https://en.wikipedia.org/wiki/You_Don%27t_Own_Me
(https://en.wikipedia.org/wiki/You_Don't_Own_Me)

Are You a Control Freak Quiz, used by permission Dr. Karl Albrecht
Ph.D. BrainSnacks. June 22, 2010.
https://www.psychologytoday.com/us/blog/brainsnacks/2010
06/are-you-control-freak-take-quiz-and-find-out

Chapter 9:
Sorry About That!

Love Story Movie: Paramount Pictures, 1970, based on a *Love Story*
book by Erich Segal.

Ten Boom, Corrie, Forgiveness quote:
https://www.goodreads.com/author/quotes/102203.Corrie_ten
_Boom
Gone with the Wind: Think about it tomorrow's quote. International
Pictures, 1939 adapted from the novel by Mitchell, Margaret.
Chapman, Gary, Thomas, Jennifer: *5 Languages of an Apology.*
September 2006, Northfield Publishing.

Chapter 10:
Are You Mad at Me Too, God?

Britten, Terry, Lyle, Graham writers. *What's Love Got to Do With it? Sung by* Tina Turner, 1984, Capitol Records.

Final Words:
So, What's a Girl to DO, Now?

Bright, Bill: Taken from *The 4 Spiritual Laws* Booklet. Bright Media Foundation/Campus Crusade for Christ International, 1965.

Made in the USA
Monee, IL
26 September 2020

42816935R00118